Working With Dreams
A Handbook of Techniques

Joan C. Harthan, PhD

Cover photograph: Dovestone Reservoir, Saddleworth © Joan C. Harthan
Artwork & Photographs © Joan C. Harthan

ISBN: 1-4839-4248-1
ISBN-13: 978-1483942483

CONTENTS

ACKNOWLEDGMENTS

This book is a collection of dream analysis techniques acquired over twenty five years. Some of them are tried and tested and have been in general use for a long time. Some are relatively new techniques that I've adapted or modified over the years. Where possible I've given credit to the originator of the technique but it hasn't always been possible to do this; methods evolve and change over time or are adapted to suit different situations. I apologise if I've omitted to acknowledge an individual's contribution; this has not been intentional. Some of the techniques are uniquely associated with their originator, in which case this is clearly stated.

PART ONE

1. Introduction

Dreams provide a powerful path to self awareness. They are as much a part of our life experience as everyday reality and yet most people in the Western world ignore them, or treat them as curiosities. I've been working with my own and other people's dreams for over twenty five years and experience has taught me that dreams contain information that can be put to a number of uses; all of them valuable and all of them potentially life changing. Working with our dreams challenges us to open up to the possibility that there may be things inside us of which we are not consciously aware. This may be aspects of our life or behavior, or it may be a dormant talent that has been denied expression. We have all bought into a program of limitation, presented to us as children. The beliefs we learned before we were six years old are so ingrained that we believe they're a part of our genetic makeup. They're not, but you can't eliminate these beliefs unless you know what they are and how they are affecting your life. Once uncovered, you need to be willing to discard them. And therein lies the problem; the carbuncle of successful dream work. Limitations and boundaries, although confining us like the walls of a prison, can make us feel safe. We're in familiar territory; in our comfort zone. The knowledge of what lies beneath this facade often remains undiscovered because, on some level, we know that its emergence will upset the apple cart. It can jolt us out of our safe haven. We may have to learn new rules, new ways of being in the world. We may have no choice but to face up to those challenges that our ego has always tried to avoid. If we change and the people around us don't, what are we to do then? It's for all these reasons, and more besides, that dream interpretation can be so very difficult. Our ego has built a fortress around its self-image and it won't allow the walls to fall down without a fight. Take for instance the man who had a 'silly dream about nothing in particular'. After using one of the techniques in this book, he realized that an underlying health problem was the result of stress at work. As his job defined who he was, and he had always maintained that he could cope with any amount of stress, he was faced with a difficult decision. Should he quit or should he continue to enjoy his status at the expense of his health?

For better or worse, this is what the techniques in this book are designed to do; overcome the ego censorship and stir memories and ideas within the unconscious. They are the only tools you need in order to work productively with dreams. Each technique has step by step instructions that can be used by individuals in their own home, one-on-one in professional counseling or therapy, or by groups; whether dream groups, schools and colleges or corporate businesses.

You'll find a comprehensive index (APPENDIX I) at the back of the book, which shows, at a glance, which techniques are suitable for which situation. Most of the techniques can be adapted for use in any environment but the tick boxes give an indication of where each technique may be best employed. If you are a therapist or a counselor, you'll find they offer structured, yet simple and flexible, methods for incorporating dream work into your practice.

Dream interpretation is more than entertainment. Dreams can be used to make life better if we take the time to understand them; nurture them; honor them. It's amazing how even just one dream can empower us to take action in our everyday life; action we may not otherwise have considered. Dreams offer creative solutions to problems. They can give us the confidence to make the right life choice, whether that's making the right decision about which path to take, which relationships to nurture and which to let go of, or informing us of our hidden gifts and talents. When they warn us of developing health problems, they can even save our life. Working with dreams doesn't have to be particularly onerous or time consuming. It's tremendous fun to share dreams and comforting to remember that, in almost every culture, our ancestors shared their dreams every day.

The peace and happiness we all seek is attainable. You'll find the signposts in your dreams, all you have to do is stay on the road.

2. Exploring Your Dreams

Whichever technique you use to explore your dreams, there are a few 'rule of thumb' guidelines that can be applied in all instances. If you're short of time, these guidelines can be used alone to give a quick overview of a dream. However, they will not give the depth of insight you will get from using the techniques.

KEY POINTS ABOUT DREAMS

- ALWAYS assume that a dream has a meaning.

- Dreams never come to tell us what we already know; they always contain new insights.

- Recognize that you must LEARN the language of dreams – dreams speak to us in metaphor and symbols.

- Dreams are almost always about a current life issue.

- To understand your dreams you must learn the skill of EXPLORING them and be prepared to venture outside the boundaries of your comfort zone.

- Most dreams reflect the way your 'inner self' is experiencing life events. The inner self goes by many different names; unconscious/spirit/soul/higher self/the divine aspect. It doesn't matter what you call it, the language it uses is still the same.

- Don't discount the possibility that some dreams contain transpersonal elements. There is growing evidence that other people, both living and dead, communicate with us through our dreams.

- Be open to the possibility that some dreams might be real communications from the spiritual realm or, if you prefer, real contact with the energy field that Physicists now believe connects all things on the quantum level. If you've ever had a lucid dream, that's a dream where you know you are dreaming, you've probably already considered this possibility. However, my advice is to explore all dreams on a personal level initially.

General 'Rule of Thumb' Advice

- Whichever technique you are using, always ask yourself "Why?" Why that particular symbol and not something else? Why was I driving a red car and not a blue truck?

- Illogical events, conflicts and inconsistencies are always good clues to the meaning of the dream. Your first port of call should be to try and identify a similar situation in your life.

- Pay particular attention to large things in your dreams or things that are emphasized in some way. For instance, if you're being chased by a giant you can be sure whatever it is you're running away from is a big problem.

- Pay attention to any colors that stand out, they will invariably be important clues as to which emotion prompted the dream.

- Empower yourself as the final authority on your dream. If someone tries to tell you what your dream means, explain politely that, whilst you appreciate their help, their interpretation reveals more about them than it does about you.

RECORDING YOUR DREAMS

- It helps if you get into the habit of writing your dreams down immediately you wake up.

- If you can, record dreams in the PRESENT TENSE. This puts you back into the energy of the dream.

- Give your dream a TITLE.

- Record the feeling where the emotion seems to be the strongest.

- Dreams use metaphorical language to tell their stories and employ symbolism as a means of expressing complex ideas and thoughts. Explore the metaphors and the symbols in all your dreams.

- After working on a dream, record your findings alongside the dream.

- Avoid judging the relevance of a dream before you've explored it. It's the ego that makes the judgment and this can close your mind to other possible meanings. Even simple, mundane dreams often hold very important messages.

- Follow up the dream. When you've arrived at an understanding, ask yourself, "Is there any action I can take to incorporate the message of the dream into my life?" If so, DO IT. The action you take can be as important as making a major life change or as simple as wearing the same color dress you were wearing in the dream.

3. Sharing Your Dreams

A few dos and don'ts

As a member of the International Association for the Study of Dreams, I take ethical issues very seriously. I've seen too many instances where a dream has been shared and the dreamer is left wishing they hadn't shared it. Whether you're working alone, one-to-one or in a group, if you are alert to this danger, you will be in a position to voice gentle reminders about privacy and safety.

Dreams were always meant to be shared. Dream sharing opens new doors into our dreams and our psyche; doors that may be we hadn't seen or our egos are pretending don't exist. But dream sharing can be risky, dealing as it does with immensely personal issues. We may not want to divulge personal information, and we may not want people invading our privacy by asking prying questions about our personal life. It can also be exceedingly irritating, and sometimes upsetting, to have someone else tell you what your dream means. What they're actually doing is voicing their opinion about the issues in your life. They snatch your dream away and claim all the power for themselves. This is not acceptable. So, it's important to recognize that no one can possibly understand the true meaning of a dream except the dreamer. Dream ownership is not transferable.

Group work

Crossing boundaries in dream work is an ever-present danger that dream facilitators have to be on their guard against. Staying within ethical boundaries is the top priority of any dream group. Participants in dream work, particularly group dream work, need to feel safe and secure. If other people's comments make them feel judged or psychically violated, it can have devastating consequences. Jeremy Taylor gives a charter to each participant in his dream work groups. It lays down basic ground rules that all participants must adhere to. This Dreamwork Tool Kit is freely available on his website for those who wish to use it.

The aim of group work is to help the dreamer explore their dream, not to make assumptions about what the dream might mean. It is, therefore, not necessary for the dreamer to divulge any personal information at all. They can do so if they wish but should not be made to feel under any obligation, and under no circumstances should they be asked questions about their personal life.

Any comments or questions about the dream should be objective and stay within the boundaries of the dream. For instance; if the dream was about the dreamer taking something without permission, you may ask, "How did you feel in the dream when you took this thing?" and not, "Have you ever stolen anything in real life?"

A comment on the 'If this were my dream' scenario.

This is a widely used, and abused, method of working with dreams in a group situation. It was a method devised by Montague Ullman and, when used correctly and ethically, as it was intended, is an excellent way to help the dreamer explore their dream. Unfortunately it is often used as a cover for telling someone else what their dream means and what they should do about it.

It involves the active participation of the listener, who is free to bring in any associations, feelings or memories that the dream suggests to them, including dreams of their own that may contain similar themes. Whatever they say must be preceded with, "If this were my dream . . . ". For example: if the dreamer has related a dream in which she is conversing with someone who seems to be dressed in her husband's clothes, the listener may recall a similar dream of their own. Perhaps the listener, after working on their own dream, understands that people we know are sometimes disguised in our dreams as someone else. This dream experience may lead them to say, "If it were my dream, I would like to go back into the dream and ask the person why they are wearing my husband's clothes". In this way, they would be suggesting some action the dreamer could take to further explore their dream. If, however, their response is, "If it were my dream I'd assume that my husband is hiding something from me," this is clearly crossing the boundary of what is acceptable. The difference between these two responses is clear. One empowers the dreamer, the other tells the dreamer that they have problems in their marriage, which may or may not be true.

Dream sharing is a sharing of experience and knowledge in an equal partnership. Nothing more. When it's done correctly, it's a very powerful method. The comments and insights provided by other people, even strangers, can be tremendously important in encouraging us to consider all possible aspects of our dream.

Here are the rules of the game:

- Never, ever presume to tell someone what their dream means.

- Comments must be confined to what the dream would mean if it were your dream. Understand that your comments will say more about you than they say about the dreamer.

- Any comments about the dream should be addressed to the group, not to the dreamer. Avoid eye contact with the dreamer, this makes it impersonal and emphasizes the point that this is YOUR view on what the dream might mean when applied to YOUR life situation not theirs.

4. Dreams As A Therapeutic Tool

I suspect that the number of professional therapists who use their patient's dreams as part of the therapeutic process is quite low. This may be because the importance of dreams is generally not recognized in academically accredited training programs, at least not in the UK. But whilst there is reluctance on the part of some academically trained professional therapists to make use of clients' dreams, there are many self-styled therapists that do, and usually very successfully.

If this is something you don't currently incorporate into your practice, let me explain why it may be a good idea to do so. Dreams can facilitate exploration of an issue in a way that is non-threatening. Often one of the most difficult obstacles to overcome is the barrier of denial that the client presents. If the therapist moves too quickly, the client can feel threatened and close up completely. Using a dream to focus on, can reduce this difficulty to something more manageable. During, or after, the exploration of the dream the person undergoing therapy can be invited to discuss why they think they had the dream and what it might be saying about their present situation. In this way, they are fully engaged in the therapeutic process. They are empowered to take control of the issues that are causing them distress without feeling coerced into confronting them.

Some therapists are inclined to use only one professionally recognized approach in their practice. This can be helpful in guiding the client to an understanding of their problem and giving them confidence in the practitioner. However, care must be taken not to try and convince the client of the authenticity of a particular psychological theory in order to reinforce their own philosophy. It may lead the dreamer to feel they should accept a dream meaning that they are not wholly comfortable with, or even fully understand. It's much better if the dreamer is allowed to come to their own understanding without feeling that their lack of knowledge compromises their judgment. In other words, therapists must guard against the tendency of the client to see the therapist as an authority on the meaning of their dream.

End of Life Counseling

The 1990s saw the appearance of articles and research papers in Nursing Journals that dealt with the utilization of dreams as a way of approaching and discussing the issues that a dying person must face. Preparation for death is not something the western world is very good at and often the dying person is unable, or unwilling, to discuss their feelings or their fears. Having a dream to discuss, focuses the issues that are troubling them and makes those issues easier to accept and resolve. In this way dreams help people circumvent their denial of what's happening to them and can help them accept the inevitable. The beauty of using dreams is that it can be approached in a casual way. Perhaps after telling the dying person one of your own dreams, ask them, "Do you ever dream?" This will often result in them telling you a recent dream that may have been troubling them. I'm relieved to report that there is now a lot of work being done in this area and there are many caring practitioners helping people in this way.

Life Transitions

Death is but one transition we all must face in our lifetime. Assimilating and integrating major changes such as puberty, parenthood and old age can be just as challenging. These transitions used to be marked with ceremony and guidance. In secular societies, especially in the developed countries, these transitions are no longer integrated in a way that is healthy for our society or for our spiritual well-being. People are left to cope as best they can. Perhaps the Western pre-occupation with remaining youthful is a result of this lack. It sends out a message that growing old is a negative life condition that should be halted if at all possible. What a shame we don't recognize that increasing age can bring with it wisdom and compassion and an increasing desire for peace and plenty for everyone. It is well-documented that dreams occurring during life transitions, if brought into consciousness and explored, can result in a healthy assimilation of the changes being experienced. This brings with it a willingness to let go of the past whilst fostering a positive expectation about the future.

5. Taking Dream Work Into Schools

Dreaming is a universal phenomenon and most children have an inherent fascination about what dreams mean. So why not make dream work part of the school curriculum? Not only does it develop communication and social skills but it can provide a bridge to all other subject areas. Dreams, being imaginal expressions of our feelings and our concerns, can teach students to understand metaphorical language enabling them to move from concrete to more abstract and creative ways of thinking. This will not only give them a greater understanding of Art and Literature but also the hard sciences, where abstract concepts can be conveyed clearly and concisely using analogy or metaphor. In addition, students will begin to know themselves much better. They will have the opportunity to discover their strengths and weaknesses, their hang ups and their beliefs. This discovery will result in increased self-awareness which will foster self-empowerment, self-esteem and a feeling of self-responsibility. In addition, dreams can provide ideas for future goals and self-development.

Dreams also contain enormous creative potential and have been used as a unique resource by writers and artists for thousands of years. Students will acquire a sense of their own individual creativity. The benefits to be gained in creative pursuits are obvious, for instance creative writing and artwork, but creative solutions are often needed to solve scientific problems, especially in research. Many scientific breakthroughs have been the result of people recognizing, in their dreams, the answer they were seeking.

There are also huge social benefits to be had from exploring dreams in the classroom. We often find personal relevance in other people's dreams. It helps us to recognize that, as human beings, we share the same emotions and have similar fears. This can lead to a better understanding and tolerance of other people. Group work in schools provides an ideal vehicle for listening to, and understanding, many different viewpoints and life situations. The outcome of this is that a feeling of empathy is fostered and students are less likely to project their inner conflicts onto the outside world and engage in destructive behavior. In other words, sharing dreams leads to a more caring, empathetic society. We all have enormous unrealized potential and with that the ability to make a difference in the world around us. Students can be made aware of this potential by engaging in dream studies.

For adolescents and older students, any of the techniques presented in this book can be used to great effect. For younger children I suggest a more holistic approach by including an exploration of sleep and sleep patterns. In APPENDIX II you'll find details of two sessions I devised for UK Key Stage 2 children, (ages seven to eleven). The sessions were very enjoyable for both myself and the children, who produced some marvelous work. Please feel free to use this plan in your own work, all I ask is that you reference the source.

PART TWO

Thirty Techniques

1
A GOOD STORY: PLOT ANALYSIS

Any professional writer will tell you that good plots have their foundation in characterization and conflict, reflecting human emotions that are identifiable to the reader. A good story has a definite **Theme** centered around some sort of **Conflict**. As the story unfolds, the conflict reaches a **Climax**, (i.e. things can't get any worse) and this results in the hero/heroine acting in such a way as to **Resolve** the conflict. In addition to the main plot, stories often contain sub-plots peripheral to the main action, these add extra dimensions and more interest. They too will have an identifiable Theme, Conflict, Climax and (possibly) Resolution. Reviewing your dream as if it were a work of fiction is a fun thing to do and will show you that most dreams are quite adept at telling a good story. It will also help you evaluate your dream more objectively, and that can lead to deep insight.

Unlike works of fiction, however, some dreams taken alone may seem to be incomplete, especially if they don't offer a resolution to the conflict. Often this is because the subconscious is dealing with a real life soap opera, which is being presented in installments as the life situation develops and unfolds. So, in the absence of an identifiable resolution, it's likely that the subconscious has not yet finished mulling over this particular problem.

As the majority of dreams are anxiety dreams and all anxiety dreams have, at their root, some sort of conflict, you'll never be short of dreams to work on using this technique. The conflict may be internal, perhaps you are being forced to act in a way that is contrary to your nature, or it may be a conflict with another person that is adversely affecting your life in some way. Whatever the reason, this technique will be useful in discovering the cause and effect and has the potential to offer a resolution.

WHAT YOU'LL NEED

Paper & pen

INSTRUCTION

Step 1

Imagine your dream is a stage play or TV drama, and you have been asked to review it for a blog post. Begin your review by writing a synopsis about the place where the dream occurs. Identify the characters and the props, and note any resemblances to things or situations in your waking life.

Step 2

Read the dream through very carefully a number of times and identify the development of the plot(s) and the associated developing tensions. How many plots and sub-plots are there? Within each subplot identify, and make notes on, the Theme and the Conflict. Next, identify the climax that follows the appearance of each conflict; this is the culmination of the tension that has been building. Something decisive happens or changes occur. The climax may appear almost immediately or may be separated from the conflict by another sub-plot. Finally look for any resolutions or outcomes, i.e. the way in which the dreaming self has resolved the conflict. Bear in mind that resolutions do not always result in happy endings and the outcome may be something you find abhorrent or distasteful. If this is the case, remember that we don't always like what's best for us! The absence of a resolution usually indicates that the conflict has not yet been resolved in the subconscious and so you may choose to seek a solution on a conscious level.

Step 3

Once you have dissected your dream in this way, you need to try and identify to which area of your life it relates, with specific reference to the emotion that underlies the conflict(s). You can then decide whether the dream contains an acceptable resolution to your current situation. If it does, then you can act on this in your waking life. If it doesn't, try asking yourself how you would like the story to end. What would need to happen for this story to come to a satisfactory conclusion?

2
ASSOCIATIVE TECHNIQUE

This technique involves uncovering the associations you have to the symbols or images in your dream. It was a method used by both Freud and Jung. Freud encouraged his clients to make associations with each successive word until the associations dried up. Jung, however, believed that this can cause the dreamer to go off at a tangent, away from the meaning of the dream. He continually brought his client back to the dream symbol rather than allowing them to lose sight of it and become lost in associations which in the end may have nothing to do with the dream meaning. You can use either of these approaches.

The idea is that you allow your mind free rein to verbalize associated ideas, words or emotions in order to unlock the symbolic meaning. It's important to remember that feelings about words or images are just as important and you must say the first thing that comes into your head, e.g. mattress on the floor may prompt words like dirty, poverty, squatters which may then lead to feelings of disgust or pity etc...

This technique can be useful to uncover symbolism born from past experiences. For example, the image of a black dog may prompt you to remember a time when you were frightened of being bitten by such a dog. This would suggest that the dog in the dream may represent something that is hurting or frightening you in the present. Everything in a dream is there for a reason and has an association with the thought process that prompted the dream to occur. These associations are often hard for the conscious mind to recognize but nothing is chosen at random. The more prominent the symbol, the more important it will be and the more likely it is to provide you with a clue to the dream message.

WHAT YOU'LL NEED

Pen and paper.

Voice Recorder (optional).

INSTRUCTION

Step1
Write down the dream you are going to work on in as much detail as you can, and in the present tense.

Step 2
Jot down a few notes about which life situation you think the dream is addressing.

Step 3
Pick out the key images and symbols and write each one at the top of its own column on a blank sheet of paper. If you are not sure which components of the dream story constitute the symbols, they are usually identifiable as the nouns.

Step 4
Starting with the first symbol, write down, underneath the relevant column heading, all the associations (feelings or images) that spring to mind directly from that particular word. It doesn't have to be just one word; it can be all the feelings or emotions associated with a word or concept. If you're struggling to make any associations, imagine you are describing its appearance and function to someone from another planet. For instance, how would you describe a chair? It's got four legs to make it stable. People sit in it when they're tired, eating, talking etc... Doing this will usually get you thinking more laterally and stir your own memories and associations. If working alone, you may find it easier to use a Voice Recorder and make your written notes afterwards. If working with a partner, they can jot down what you say during the exercise. These notes can be used to further explore the dream meaning later.

Step 5
Study your completed columns of words. Does anything spring to mind? How do you feel? Does what you are reading remind you of

anything going on currently in your waking life? Try and think 'outside the box'. Unconscious thought processes make connections laterally and so the connections may be hard for your conscious mind to find. Persevere. Do any of the symbols need amplifying? (See the explanation below). If so, go and do some background research about them and relate this back to the dream and your waking situation.

Step 6

Try and sum up the meaning of the dream in one sentence.

Step 7

Do you need to take any action? If so, what?

Amplification.

This is a way of obtaining more information about a symbol. It involves researching the cultural associations and relating the information gained back to the dream. How does it help you understand the life situation? For instance, I dreamed of an owl in the same room as a cat. It prompted me to buy the book 'The Owl and the Pussycat' and to explore how the message in that story related to my dream and my life. Because the dreaming mind operates outside of our waking cognition, you will usually find that such non-personal information is directly related to the area of life your dream is addressing.

Blue Handbag	Red Bus	Cobbled Street

3
BOOK OF THE DREAM

They say there's a book in everyone, but where to start and what to write about? This technique is all about compiling a book about one particular dream that you know instinctively was important. Making a book by hand is a very fulfilling way to express the creativity of a dream and is a powerful tool for self-discovery. Its function is not necessarily for interpretation but as a medium by which we can gain an insight into ourselves. It's an on-going project that will become a labor of love. As your book grows and develops, it will deepen the dream experience and lead to more insights over time. Often it will become a record of spiritual enlightenment or evolution; a landmark journey into self-discovery. If you feel more ambitious and have been recording your dreams for a while you could choose a dream theme rather than an individual dream for the subject of your book. For instance; you may have had a number of dreams with a similar theme and these dreams, when collected together, would provide immense insight into your psyche. Dreams of running away from something, for example, could be collected together into a book entitled, "Why I want to run away".

WHAT YOU'LL NEED

Use anything that you think is appropriate. You'll be combining images, words and experiences from the dream and also from your life; past, present and future. Initially you will need to decide on the type of base material you are going to use for your book. It is possible to purchase attractively bound notebooks quite cheaply but if you do this, make sure the paper is of good quality. You may prefer to use a scrapbook or even a loose-leaf binder. Whatever you choose, make sure it is durable, of good quality and is attractive. You'll also need writing and drawing materials, perhaps even scraps of fabric for collage work. You will also need to be on the lookout for pictures, photographs, magazine articles and anything else that appertains to your dream.

You'll be surprised at what presents itself once you have set your intention.

INSTRUCTION

Step 1
The way in which you set out your book is part of the creative process and so I am not offering any suggestions for layout and structure. This will depend on the nature of the dream and also on your own style and preferences. The important thing is to plan the book out beforehand; this is especially important if using a bound notebook. A rough framework plan will help to order your thoughts and ideas although it's not necessary to stick with this plan. As you progress with the book, you must allow it to grow and evolve in accordance with its own demands. Begin by collecting together any information or material you feel is appropriate.

Step 2
Begin your book by writing down your dream(s). Give the dream(s) a title. Apply some of the techniques in this book and record all your discoveries.

Step 4
You'll uncover more source material as time passes. Each time you add to the book, keep the dream in mind, immerse yourself in it totally and, in the weeks ahead, keep your eyes and ears open for events or symbols in your everyday life that seem to relate to the dream. These could take the form of signs or omens in nature, or perhaps something someone says, or even something you see on the TV or internet.

Step 5
Your book can be continually added to; perhaps by adding dreams with the same theme or by recording real life events or experiences that occur in the weeks or years following the dream. You could also use your dream as the starting point for psychic questing, (see explanation below); using the book to record your research findings and subsequent

experiences. You could also use it for a piece of creative writing. There is no limit as to how you can develop this work and it may well turn into a lifelong project. There are no rules except that you must be creative, and inquisitive and, most importantly, be very proud of your Book of the Dream.

Psychic Questing

A modern day Psychic Quester is Andrew Collins whose experiences and adventures can be found in his books and on his website. His definition of the term is, "using intuitively inspired thoughts and information (*including dreams*) for creative purposes, be it the exploration of history, the search for hidden artifacts or simply the quest for enlightenment", *(my italics)*.

4
BOX OF DREAMS

This is a really useful technique to use if you're struggling to make sense of the images or symbols in your dream. It can also be put to good use as a trigger for creative writing. Teachers will find it an exciting and stimulating method to use in the classroom, especially with younger children. It involves engaging all the senses in an imaginary, physical exploration of the things contained in the dream.

If at first you find the method difficult, don't give up. With practice it will become easier and you'll probably find yourself engaging your five senses more fully in your everyday life. This can only add to the enjoyment of your life experience. Thanks to Clare Johnson for sharing this technique with the International Association for the Study of Dreams.

WHAT YOU'LL NEED

Pen, coloured pencils and paper.

A cardboard box, preferably sealed, with a hole in one side big enough to put your hand through.

Voice Recorder (optional).

Access to the internet and/or magazines containing lots of colour pictures (optional).

INSTRUCTION

Step 1

Choose a selection of images or symbols from your dream. They need not all be mysterious or intriguing, everyday images work just as well. Make sure you have a good sense of them and, if possible, get a concrete representation of them. For instance; if I dream of a fire I could paint or draw a representation of it, or even download and print out an image of a fire from the World Wide Web.

Step 2

Choose one of the images and pop it into the box. Make sure you have a pen and paper handy or, if using a Voice Recorder, make sure it's switched on. Now put your hand inside the box, keep your eyes closed initially.

Step 3

Imagine you are touching the thing that the image represents. What does it feel like? What is its temperature? Is it moving? What does it communicate to you? Record what you experience, keeping your notes brief with lots of verbs and adjectives, (doing and describing words).

Step 4

Now put your nose to the hole and sniff. Engage your imagination fully. What does it smell like? Does the smell remind you of anything? Again, record your experiences.

Step 5

Now put your ear to the hole and listen to it. Is it making a noise? Is it talking/whining/singing? What is it saying? Take notes.

Step 6

Now put your mouth to the hole and stick out your tongue. What does it taste like? Sweet/bitter/salty? Try and be very specific. Record what you experience.

Step 7

Take the image out of the box and hold it. Feel it in your arms as if it were real. Is it moving? How is it moving? Is it heavy or light? Does it have feelings? Is it happy/sad/angry? How does it feel about you? Has it got a message for you?

Step 8

Now drop it on the floor. What happens to it? Does it explode? Turn into something else? Break? Run away?

Step 9

Repeat these steps with every image you selected.

Step 10

Review your notes. Hopefully you've recorded/written lots of short lines, such as 'its voice is fizzing', 'it's hiding in some lavender', 'its tongue is tangled round mine.' Use these notes to do some creative writing. For example, with the notes above you may write; 'It fizzed as it hid in the lavender and spoke of lives touching in a tangle of tongues'. Perhaps write a poem or a piece of Flash Fiction. If you want to write a poem, why not use the format of Kit Wright's poem 'The Magic Box' in which each verse has four lines, and each verse begins with the words 'I will put in the box'. Here's an example:

MY BOX OF DREAMS

I will put in the box
Death, my silent teacher,
With dry bones and parched skin
On a head of nails.

I will put in the box
A curling, golden serpent, silky smooth,
With rose colored breath
Hissing at a tornado of tears.

I will put in the box
A wriggling, twiggling, mouse
With warm nose twitching
Beckoning the Buddha to play.

Step 11

Relate your experiences, your notes and your creative writing to something going on in your life. What have you discovered? Is there any action you can take to bring the message of the dream into your life?

Step 12

To illustrate your dream or your piece of writing, why not draw your Box of Dreams?

5
DOUBLE D - DOING & DESCRIBING

The first technique in this book, the Associative Technique, looks at the symbols and images in a dream. These are mainly the nouns, the things that we can see and describe easily. A different technique is to focus on the verbs, adverbs and adjectives that we've used to record the dream. This approach quickly draws out the emotional content of a dream and its true meaning is less vulnerable to self-deception. It's useful for ascertaining the situation that gave rise to the dream and the message can often be revealed with very little effort.

What are verbs, adverbs and adjectives?

- *verbs* are the "doing" words that convey the action, or state of being. They can be past, present or future tense. For example:
    - ✓ I **ran** to the forest (past)
    - ✓ I **feel** warm (present)
    - ✓ I will **leave** soon (future)
- *adverbs* are used to modify a verb, an adjective or another adverb. They are added to another word to express some modification of the meaning or an accompanying circumstance. For example:
    - ✓ I spoke **loudly** (modifies the verb *spoke*)
    - ✓ I was **very** cross with him (modifies the adjective *cross*)
    - ✓ I was speaking **too** quickly (modifies the adverb *quickly*)
- *adjectives* are descriptive words that qualify a noun (person, place, object or idea) or pronoun (he, she, her, him etc...). It describes size, colour, how many, which one, whose or what kind. For example:
    - ✓ The **old** woman stroked a **black** cat as she pointed her **bony** finger at the **little** girl.

Here's an example of how all these are included in one sentence:
I was **running** *(verb)* **away from** *(adverb)* a **huge** *(adjective)* tiger.

WHAT YOU'LL NEED

Paper & pen. Two pens of different colors will be useful; highlighter pens are ideal.

INSTRUCTION

Step 1
Highlight or underline what you feel are the most important verbs and accompanying adverbs in one color, and all the adjectives and accompanying adverbs in a different color.

Step 2
Make two lists of all the highlighted words in color coded columns so you have a list of all the action (verbs) and a list of all the descriptions (adjectives) with their accompanying adverbs.

Step 3
Examine the verbs in the action column. Does anything spring to mind? Take the words out of the context of the dream; is this action you've taken or are contemplating taking in everyday life? If so, you can be sure this is what the dream is about.

Step 4
Examine the adjectives in the description column. What emotions do these words stir in you? Connect these words/emotions to what you discovered in Step 3.

Step 5
Make careful notes about how the dream is portraying the situation under review. If you need further insight you can move onto the nouns (characters, symbols and images) connected to those actions or feelings.

Step 6
Decide what is the dream's message? Does the dream suggest a course of action? If so what? Is there any other action you could take?

6
DREAM ANIMALS

In this technique we will work with animal energies to bring about positive change in our life. Between 5 and 10% of all adult dreams contain an animal. Sometimes it's a living pet, sometimes a pet from our past, sometimes it's a wild animal that we've never seen in real life. In the Shamanic tradition, animals embody the energy of their species. This energy is very specific and can be tapped into and drawn into your life by experiencing and identifying with the animal. So, for instance, if I need more energy I may dream about a Horse (horsepower), and contemplation of the energy displayed by horses will help to draw Horse energy into my sphere of being. If I need to slow down and retreat into my own space for a while to take stock of things, I may dream of Tortoise. Tortoise speaks of self-reliance and self-determination with slow, considered action.

Animals that threaten us in our dreams are the embodiment of our fears. They are connected to a fear that already exists and has its roots in some traumatic or fearful experience in our personal history or in the history of our species. The animal that threatens us may be an aspect of our character (often instinctual in nature) that we may be repressing, or that is getting out of control. Our instinct, when faced with such a threat in real life, is to either fight or flee and the reaction of our dreaming self is often the same. However, when we run away from things, we give away some of our power to them and this makes them stronger, and ultimately even harder to overcome. A hostile, fearsome dream animal is powerful enough without us giving him even more power over us. By befriending the animal and understanding its nature, it is possible to overcome our fear of whatever it is that is preventing us from living our lives to the full.

Because dreams are a reflection of how we are experiencing the world, one of the common motifs in the dreams of people suffering emotional pain, is of a wounded animal. This feeling of being wounded often manifests into our waking reality as feelings of depression or helplessness. We may find ourselves unable to think positively about the future and this will draw even more negative energy to us. In such cases, focusing our thoughts on healing our dream animal, whilst recognizing that this animal is an aspect of our self, can be an extremely powerful pathway to self-healing and self-love.

Quite often we fail to understand, on a conscious level, what certain animals mean to us and it's only when we investigate the Shamanic associations that we realize how appropriate this animal is to our present situation. This is part of the magic that weaves its way into dream work.

WHAT YOU'LL NEED

Recording medium, whether paper and pen or a Voice Recorder.

A dream animal to work with.

INSTRUCTION

Step 1
Choose a dream where an animal appeared. Write down, in as much detail as you can, what the animal was doing, what state of health it was in, did it speak to you/look at you/touch you/chase you/attack you?

Step 2
Obtain a picture of the animal, as close a representation of the dream animal as you can get. It's a wonderful meditation to draw or paint your dream animal if you've time to do this, otherwise downloading an image from the World Wide Web is an excellent substitute. The picture of the leopard that follows these instructions is a drawing I made of one of my own dream animals.

Step 3
Find out as much about the animal as you can. It's habitat, the way it moves, what it eats etc... What is its nature? How does it care for its young? Is it a predator or is it preyed upon?

Step 4

Consult various Shamanic sources to find out what they have to say about the energy embodied by this particular animal. Bear in mind that animals act only on instinct; they are neither good nor bad. Remember too that even the most seemingly vile creatures can embody life changing messages. The medicine carried by Cockroach is just as important as that carried by Tiger.

Step 5

Now comes the exciting part; the shape shifting. I want you to become the animal. Move like it, sound like it. For instance, if it's a tiger get down on all fours and prowl around the room, looking this way and that with your hunters eyes. If you've the confidence to do this outdoors, so much the better. Are you snarling or purring? Do whatever your dream animal was doing. What is its purpose? Where is it going? What does it want? How does it feel to be your dream animal? Let the animal's voice flow through you. Does it have a message for you? Why is it here? Be prepared for anything! If you're too embarrassed to do this alone, get a friend to join you; though don't let your hilarity divert you from your task. It's also a great activity to do in group work, with everyone shape-shifting into their own dream animal.

Step 6

Whilst still in the animal form, think about the animal in the context of the dream. Why has this animal come to you? What healing does it offer? What energy is it bringing? How can it help you in a present situation? Is it telling you something about yourself or your life? Are you comfortable in this animal's skin? If not, why not? In what area of your life are you in contact with this sort of energy?

Step 7

When you feel you've got all the information you need, bring yourself back to your own body and make any notes you feel necessary. In the days to come, try and integrate the animal energy into your life and everyday tasks. Do things that will honor and satisfy the animal. For instance, if it was Tiger go for walks in the countryside, have a steak for your dinner, feel the power of Tiger growing within you.

Step 8
Working with animal energies in this way will enable you to identify your own Power Animal, and draw on its energy as and when needed. However, not all animals that come to us are Power Animals. Be discerning. If the animal energy feels good and empowers you to be a better, stronger person then go with it. Remember too that Power Animals come and go, they may stay with you for years or only days.

Leopard brings speed and an ability to work towards a goal with deadly accuracy. He's agile and aware of every detail around him.

7
DREAM DETECTIVE

This technique is sometimes known in technical jargon as the phenomenology method. It's a method to be used one-to-one, with one person interviewing the other person about their dream. The interviewer must not offer any interpretations or suggestions. They must only ask questions of the dreamer to help them explore and understand the dream.

Qualities of a good dream detective

The Dream Detective should act as an interviewer whose main goal is to HELP explore the dream experience, by guiding the dreamer to relive and/or describe the dream in more detail. Because the detective is looking objectively at the dream, it's much easier to spot contradictions and also commonalities, so be on the lookout for these and investigate them thoroughly. Ask useful questions that encourage the dreamer to think more deeply about the dream and how it relates to their life and preoccupations. The detective must be non-judgmental and supportive, whilst remaining totally impartial. Under no circumstances must they add their own comments or suggestions.

WHAT YOU'LL NEED

Pen and paper

INSTRUCTION

This is a step by step guide for the person playing the role of detective.

Step 1: Telling stage.

Ask the dreamer to tell you their dream, using first person, present tense. Whilst listening, you may find it useful to take notes in exactly the same way as a police detective would make notes when listening to a potential witness. These notes can be used as a prompt for the interview.

Step 2: Exploration stage.

The aim of this stage is to allow the dreamer to explore the dream in terms of the main images or symbols. Ask them to identify anything in their waking life that could have triggered the images. Ask the dreamer for both concrete, and associative, descriptions of the images and people in the dream. For instance:

a. **Concrete descriptions** - What did the house look like? What color was the door? Were there any steps up to the door?

b. **Associative descriptions** - How did the house make you feel? Does it remind you of a house you've been in before? You say it reminded you of your Grandmother's house, would you like to comment on the relationship you had with your Grandmother?

Step 3: Insight stage.

This stage should build on the exploration stage to arrive at a new understanding. Dreams are capable of interpretation on many levels and the dreamer should go with what feels most "right" or what seems most appropriate. This may not necessarily be an interpretation of the dream 'per se', it may be more an insight into a situation in their waking life. It's useful if the first question asked by the interviewer at this stage is, "What do you think the dream means?"

Step 4: Action stage.

By now, the dreamer should have a pretty good idea about what the dream was portraying and be clear about the area of their life that has been addressed. Ask them if this area is in need of attention or change? Ask the dreamer if they wish to discuss with you whether any action is appropriate and, if so, what form that action could take. Remind them that making a change, no matter how small, is important because it consolidates their self-examination and confirms acceptance of the dream message.

Step 5: Honor the dream.

Finally, if the dream message is important, ask the dreamer to create a physical reminder of it in their everyday life. This could be some artwork or a poem, or perhaps something bought from a shop; an ornament or perhaps a jumper of the same color as in the dream. I have a statue of an owl on my writing desk; it's a constant reminder of an encouraging and empowering dream I had many years ago about my hope that one day I would be a professional author.

8
DREAM DRAWING STORY GAME

This is an excellent, fun exercise to use in group work, especially in the classroom where students' imaginations will be stimulated. It's a method devised by Henry Reed, and was included in his book 'Getting Help From Your Dreams'.

We know more about the meaning of our dreams than we are consciously aware of, or can put into words. Our subconscious, however, having scripted them, knows exactly what they're about. Our bodies too can be very aware of the energy contained within a dream and we can often get a good understanding by letting our body do the talking. In this case, that means drawing it, preferably whilst silencing the part of us that wants to produce a work of art. Even after having disengaged our conscious mind and produced our drawing, we can find we are too intimately connected with it to appreciate what it's telling us.

To get round this, we give our drawing to someone else and, without telling them the dream, ask them to make up a story about the drawing. The other person will pick up on the clues our hands have left behind. Their story will probably not resemble the dream at all, but that doesn't matter. If we are attentive to our emotional reactions to the story as it unfolds, we might find that parts of the story, the words used or the descriptions of the characters, will trigger flashes of recognition and bring us closer to an understanding of the dream.

WHAT YOU'LL NEED

Paper, colored pencils, paints etc...

Paper for drawing and note taking.

INSTRUCTION

Step 1. Draw the dream
Have the group sitting in a circle. Invite everyone to choose a dream and draw it, in fifteen minutes, in a single picture. The purpose is not to

create a work of art but rather to express the theme, action or mood of the dream. It may be representative of the dream symbols or characters, or may be an abstract expression. It doesn't matter. Don't put any identifying marks on the drawing.

Whilst the drawing is going on, it's important there is quiet and thoughtful meditation. Also, no one must discuss or reveal the nature of the dream that's being drawn.

Step 2. Distribute the drawings

Finished drawings are collected and placed face down on the floor in the middle of the circle. Each person collects one; hopefully not knowing to whom it belongs.

Step 3. Write a story

The object of the game is not to guess what the dream was about, the purpose is to enter the drawing with imagination and emerge with a story that fits the drawing.

You can be most helpful to the dreamer if you simply let your imagination have free rein and suspend critical judgment about your story-making skills.

The story you make up must answer the following questions:

1. What's going on here?
2. What are the people, animals or things telling and thinking?
3. What led up to the present situation?
4. How does it all work out?

Allow fifteen minutes to make up a story.

Step 4. Tell the story

Each person in turns tells their story. Others may comment or obtain further details of the story but the identity of the dreamer is not revealed. If the person telling the story needs some help, that's fine, others need to be sensitive to what is going on and help if necessary. The group can offer support by asking specific questions about the drawing until a story emerges. Reassure the group that it's not the story telling skill that helps the dreamer, but rather the person's willingness to simply tell what the drawing reminds them of. Forget that it's a dream. It's a picture – what story is the picture telling? Under no circumstances should anyone make evaluative comments about the person who made the drawing. The drawing style should not come into it. If you wish, the session can end here. It has already served the purpose of giving the dreamer another perspective on their dream and also given everyone a chance to do some creative writing. However, if this is a serious dream working group that requires deeper insight, it's important that a discussion follows.

Step 5. Discussion

After the stories have been told, the dreamers are invited to identify themselves but there's no obligation to do this. If they choose to, they can tell their dream and give their reaction to the story. Discourage participants from comparing the original dream with the story, for instance: "You were right about that part." Help the dreamer with questions such as:

1. What did you learn about your dream from hearing the person's story?

2. Did the story remind you or help you become aware of any feelings you had about your dream?

3. Did the story remind you of anything about yourself?

You can also ask the storyteller to reconstruct how the drawing stimulated the story – what was most significant? Was it the color, the shading, the placement, a particular image?

There is no way of predicting what kind of insights may emerge from the discussion. It's best to allow the discussion period to be freewheeling, led by curiosity and a respect for the truth contained in feelings.

Step 6. Post-discussion

It's important that participants spend time quietly writing about the experience, preferably in a journal. The purpose is to encourage people to 'own' what they've learned. If the dreamer has found some truth in

45

the story that was written from their drawing, it's truth that's recognized from within. Writing about this will diminish any tendency to attribute the wisdom to someone else and make it easier to discard anything that doesn't ring true.

This dream was about a friendly chat in a cafe. The man has a pile of clothes on the table in front of him. The dreamer felt the dream was about her procrastination over an important decision. The person making a story about the picture saw an attempt to reconcile a domestic dispute; with the woman chastising her partner for leaving his dirty clothes lying around.

9
DREAM DUALS

It's very useful to identify glaring opposites in your dreams. The forces that are opposing each other usually underline important conflicts, or imbalances, in the life of the dreamer. The opposites can take many forms. For instance; opposite states of being, an aggressor and a victim, someone who's mobile and someone who isn't. Or it may be in the form of colors, black and white, dark and light. It may even be in the form of a situation, for instance action and non-action, awake and sleeping. There are those who believe the Universe itself has duality at its core and that this duality is reflected in all life forms and all life situations. The Eastern religions are founded on such principals, for instance the idea of yin and yang. So if you spot any duality within your dreams it's important, not only to recognize the life situation represented, but also to be aware that all opposites are part of a dynamic system that is striving for balance. The aim of this technique is to recognize the imbalances or conflicts and take action to bring them into equal balance.

WHAT YOU'LL NEED

Paper & pen and props if required.

INSTRUCTION

Step 1
Choose a dream where there is an obvious duality. Try and identify any emotion connected to the duality. Write the dream out in as much detail as you can.

Step 2
Make a visual representation of the duality. You could do this by drawing or painting a quick sketch. It doesn't have to look like the image in the dream, providing it gives you a point of focus for each of the opposites, you can represent it any way you like. You may even

want to use props or symbolic representations. For instance, if my dream was about two people arguing, one of them strong and domineering, the other soft and obliging, I may choose to represent them with a stone and a sponge. Then again, I may be happier to sketch them in their usual human form. What are they wearing? What's their body posture?

Step 3

Look carefully at your sketches. Turn them around, look at them from all angles. What do you see; really see. Jot down some descriptive words to describe them. While you're doing this, think about how they relate to your life or relationships. Which of the opposites do you think best represents you in waking life, and which represents how you feel inside; the deep emotional part of you.

Step 4

Now consider the interaction between the two objects/ideas in front of you. What would happen if they clashed? If they're tangible objects, pick them up and bang them together. What happens? What sound do they make? If they're drawings on paper, draw new sketches that show them joined together at their boundaries in different ways; perhaps from different angles. If your objects are people, you may want them to hit each other. How will they do this? Will they use a weapon or their hands? Will it be a slap in the face or a punch in the stomach?

Step 5

Once you're happy that you've covered all possible 'clashing' scenarios, try gently merging the two together What would happen if the sponge could seep into the stone, what would the new object feel like, look like? If you're working with drawings, superimpose one on top of the other in as many different ways as you can. Is one of the merged drawings more pleasing than the others? Again, if your objects are people, how could they merge? Embrace each other in a friendly gesture or in a more sexual way? Perhaps they will just shake hands? What might they say to each other?

Step 6

Having done this, are you reminded of anything that is happening or has happened in your life recently? Explore your associations to the dream symbols if you need more help to decipher this connection.

Step 7

Take the image of the merged opposites and think about how you can manifest this in your waking life. If the dream has highlighted a certain type of behavior on your part, think about what you can do in your everyday life to change that behavior or address the issue or, perhaps, heal a difficult relationship.

10
DREAM FICTION

Writing a piece of fiction from a dream is an exciting way to explore your subconscious. Many great authors and song writers throughout history have used their dreams to provide inspiration and ideas for their writing. Enid Blyton's Famous Five adventures were inspired by her dreaming life. Robert Louis Stevenson, William Blake, Charlotte Bronte, Mark Twain, Edgar Alan Poe and Graham Greene, all acknowledged the role their dreams played in the work they produced. Paul McCartney's song 'Yesterday' came to him in a dream, as did many of Billy Joel's songs. The subconscious is bursting with creative and innovative ideas; it is the writer, producer and director of some highly original stories. Dreams are initiated by our emotional response to life's problems. They deal with our fears and our passions and highlight the way in which we interact with and react to other people. Isn't this what successful writing is all about? A good story is one that the reader can identify with. Dreams are about the stuff of life, they speak of problems and aspirations that are common to the whole of humanity. Dream images are powerful because they speak with the language of the Universal unconscious - in symbols and metaphor. Your dreams can provide you with enough ideas to keep you writing for evermore. They are based on real-life situations because they reflect *your* real-life situation; all you have to do is explore the dream and then, using your writing skills, transform them into literary masterpieces! Of course, writing is a craft that is improved with practice. If you're serious about writing and have ambitions to submit your work for publication, remember that it's rare for the first draft of a story to be of a publishable standard. This is true of even the most successful writers. I would urge you, however, to keep a copy of your first draft as it's this that will be closest to the meaning of your dream.

WHAT YOU'LL NEED

Nothing but your dreams and your imagination.

INSTRUCTION

Step 1

If you don't have a complete dream to work on, any clear image or symbol from even a fleeting dream can provide ideas and inspiration.

Step 2

There are various ways of approaching the use of dreams as a creative resource. You could begin with making a list of all the important images/symbols in the dream and amplifying them to clarify their meaning and expand on the imagery. Dream Dictionaries are useful for this as they can lead you to explore aspects that you perhaps wouldn't have considered.

Step 3

Investigate and expand on your dream characters. Who are they? What are their main personality traits? What are they wearing/doing/saying? If you were standing next to them, how would you feel? Do they wear perfume? What sort of job do they do?

Step 4

Does the dream mention a specific place or time; are there historical links? All these leads should be amplified by doing some background research; the World Wide Web is an ideal medium for this sort of research.

Step 5

It will be useful to have a framework on which to hang your story. In this respect, pay special attention to the idea of cause and effect as this is a key component in story telling as it is in real life. Without cause and effect there is no story. The main character of the story will do something and this will result in a definite effect. This effect will, in turn, become the cause of a subsequent effect. These events are often readily identifiable in a dream and with a little literary license and enthusiastic embellishment can be made into an interesting story.

Step 6

If you find creative visualization easy, then one of the best methods to use is the Dream Re-entry technique. This method is especially useful if you're finding it hard to get the flow going. This is described later in the book.

Step 7

Once you've gathered all your background information, begin writing. Once you start to write, let yourself go, without worrying about grammar or punctuation. Just let the words flow and don't stop until the words dry up. If you are working from a full dream story, try and keep the dream in your mind as you write but don't feel you have to stick to it rigorously, be flexible. If you feel you've gone off at a tangent, providing the words are still flowing, what does it matter? Quite often, if this happens, it's likely that you've tapped into the storehouse of the unconscious in the place where the dream originated. For instance, an image of a beautiful, prancing horse on a conscious level may seem to be a very positive image. As your story progresses it may lead you into some conflict or trauma concerning the horse, perhaps the rider is unseated or may be the horse is killed in battle. It may be that the horse represents a deep-seated emotion that your conscious mind has chosen to ignore or repress. In this way, writing a story can be very therapeutic. You may find that the characters of the dream start to take on a role that seems to be independent of you by doing and saying unexpected things. If this happens, that's great - all you have to do is watch, listen and WRITE.

Go Fearward

Always try and identify where your energy is and draw it out as you write. All dreams deal with issues that are important to us. They are NEVER superficial; they are NEVER irrelevant. They come in the service of health and wholeness; and almost ALWAYS address issues that need resolving or are in the process of being resolved. So, whether you are simply analyzing your dreams or using them to write fiction, it's important that you recognize the underlying emotion. Sometimes you need to dig deep to discover it, but as you begin to write you will feel an emotion stirring. Go with it. Don't be afraid. Sometimes you'll get angry, sometimes you'll cry, sometimes you'll laugh. You can't write compelling fiction unless you elicit emotion from your reader and you can only do that if you're writing from direct experience. Some of the best stories were written in a rainstorm of tears.

11
THE DREAM GIFT

If you keep a Dream Diary, this exercise will be really easy. If not, you'll just have to rely on memory, which isn't a bad thing! All you need to do is amass some dream images or stories.

This exercise also works well as a group exercise.

WHAT YOU'LL NEED

Paper & pen.

Lots of dreams to work with.

INSTRUCTION

Step 1
Take a selection of dreams. If working within a group, each member tells the rest of the group one of their dreams.

Step 2
Each person individually chooses an image or a scene from each dream in the collection. You don't have to take something from every dream. Choose only the parts that resonate with you and stir some emotion within you.

Step 3
Each person then amalgamates what they've chosen to take from the dreams into a poem.

Step 4
Assemble into a poem with each verse beginning, "I give you".

Example:

Here's a poem I assembled after a week of dream work with twenty participants:

I give you
A Princess who won't leave her pyramid
And the wild boar, with courage in his eyes, who butts the door
Like a shadow that wants to be remembered.

I give you
The soft velvet feel of a butterflies wing
Beating in the tsunami of a starburst
And a mother, with warm soft breasts and a cold, hard heart.

I give you
A boy who plays with grey balloons
And a brave man in a grey uniform, who trembles inside
Whilst his ancient sage demands that he cries.

I give you all of these things
With deep respect and gratitude and love
In the hope that this heaving, rolling ocean we have voyaged together
Will wash up its fruitful bounty on all our shores.

12
DREAM MAPPING

Some dreams leave us with a very strong visual image or memory. This can be either a physical situation or environment, or something more abstract such as color, shape or emotion.

This method is a modified version of the technique originally devised by Anne Wiseman. It helps to bring the dream into consciousness and can serve as a vivid, potent reminder of what the dream was trying to tell you. If what results is somber and negative, you can change this into something more joyful by changing your Dream Map and taking positive action.

This is also a fun technique to use with young children. It's especially helpful for nightmares. By encouraging the child to draw what frightened them and then asking them to change the picture into something humorous, it shows them they have control. They may want to change the thing that frightened them into a cartoon or add a silly facial expression. Providing this is handled by the parent in a humorous way, keeping it fun and entertaining, the chances are the nightmare won't be repeated. For adults it works well if the dream map attempts to express the energy or emotion of the dream rather than being an exact representation of the dream images or story. To do this, we need to use color and shape in imaginative ways. You may end up with a very beautiful work of art!

To get in the mood and stimulate your own personal associations to different colors, look at the list of emotions below and individually assign a color to each one. There are no right or wrong answers to this. Our associations with color are not just instinctive; there are also psychological factors that affect how colors make us feel. These factors may be very personal and will often be influenced by subconscious impressions formed in emotionally charged situations; situations that may have been happy or sad.

ANGER, DESPAIR, JOY, PEACE, PASSION,

ENTHUSIASM, HATE, LOVE, FEAR, SADNESS

WHAT YOU'LL NEED

Paper & pencil & artist materials.

INSTRUCTION

Step 1

Take a few moments to recall the dream you're going to work on. Write it down in as much detail as you can, using the present tense. Concentrate on how it makes you feel. What are the emotions you experience as you examine each detail of the dream?

Step 2

Choose either a scene from the dream, a particular image or symbol, or the overall theme and translate what you're feeling into images. For instance, you may feel a deep sadness as the dreaming you explores the house you lived in as a child. What color or shape best represents this feeling? Is it a deep blue or perhaps sea green? If you could touch it, how would it feel under your hand? Soft like play dough or perhaps hard as rock? What about the house? Is it light, dark, warm, cold, welcoming, unfriendly? How can you represent this is your drawing? I find that the quicker you sketch this out on the paper, the more accurate the drawing tends to be. Don't worry about the standard of your drawing, if it's important to get a realistic representation you can always go back and concentrate on the detail afterwards. Give your map a three-dimensional feel. Consider how the components relate to each other; how will you arrange them on the paper? Will the house be on the other side of the page or will it be all around you, pervading every corner? Once you're satisfied that everything is in the right place, is the right size, right perspective, characters have the correct postures etc... start adding the color and shading. Try and faithfully reproduce the exact colors and atmosphere of the dream. The weather, environment etc... is particularly important so try and pay attention to this, think about how these things affect you on an emotional level. Once you have completed your drawing, study it, immerse yourself in it. If it could speak to you, what would it say? If it was a painting hung in an Art Gallery, how would it make you feel? Allow any thoughts, words, feelings and insights to float to the surface, without judging them. A strong image or feeling can bring emotion up out of the depths of our subconscious and clarify something which previously has only been dimly felt and not understood. Stand back from it and think about how the shapes and colors make you feel. Is it a good representation of the emotion of the dream?

Step 3

Think about how your dream relates to your waking life. Is it addressing an actual life situation or is it a fear or phobia you have carried around for many years?

Now examine your drawing, do you feel that parts are lacking something? Do you want to add something else that doesn't seem related to the dream or do you want to change some aspect of your map? Perhaps you could take those things away that seem very negative, or make you feel uncomfortable, and add shapes and colors that are lighter and more positive. It's a good idea to start a fresh drawing at this point. Give yourself free rein to do as you please. You don't have to stick to the same images but be aware of how you are changing the picture. How does whatever it is you are changing relate to your dream. Think in terms of both the emotional context and the actual symbols, characters and story of the dream. If you have identified a life situation that may have caused this dream to occur, start to think about how any changes you are making on your Dream Map could be translated into changes in the life situation.

Step 4

Once you are happy with the finished product, think, carefully, about any changes you have made and how they might suggest action you could take in your life to make your current situation, or attitude, more like the revised Dream Map and less like the original. Are these changes feasible? How will you implement them? Draw up an action plan if necessary.

Step 5

Place your pictures somewhere you will see them every day, the bathroom is ideal. Meditate on them over the next week or so. If you are struggling to understand the meaning, put them away somewhere out of sight for a while. You will most certainly have other dreams that will include some of the same dream imagery. As you continue to explore your dreams, the meanings of these images or symbols will become clearer; giving you more insight into the meaning of the original dream.

The dreamer was on a train that had derailed. Passengers were aggressive and she was in tears. She thought the dream portrayed her fear about the possibility that a new venture might fail, leaving her 'flat broke'. The revised map shows her protecting herself and her assets. She's back on track and rolling along.

13
DREAM METAPHORS

The way our subconscious processes our thoughts and experiences is likely to be by way of metaphorical association, rather than spoken language. Most dream workers agree that dreams operate in the same way and are a collection of metaphors strung together into a story. This universal language of the subconscious is capable of being understood by everyone. It is the language of poets and artists and transcends culture and race barriers.

The Dream Metaphor technique will help you identify the metaphors in your own dreams.

Common Metaphors

People sharing a common culture will, at one time or another, have used these and fully understand what they mean when they hear other people use them. Take, for example, the feeling of not being able to cope; the person may say that they feel they are *"falling apart"* or *"going to pieces"*. Their friends might say *"pull yourself together"* or *"get a grip of yourself"*. Taken literally, these statements don't make sense and yet they communicate, very well, emotions that are difficult to describe in any other way. So, it's very easy for us to express the concerns of everyday life in this way and we all do it, all of the time.

Tabooed Metaphors

George Lakoff, in his book "Metaphors We Live By", has suggested that, on a subconscious level, we also construct tabooed metaphors, which are not expressed in conventional language. Freud was largely concerned with these. He believed, for instance, that any tall and erect dream image represents the penis and any hole, passage or cave represents the womb or vagina.

Dream Metaphors

The metaphors that dreams use are not confined to those metaphors that are in common usage. Dreams more often use what are termed conceptual metaphors. These are the metaphors our subconscious produces from our own, very personal, expectations and experiences. To the conscious mind, they may seem arbitrary and incoherent. This is because they are derived from abstract thoughts using sensory-derived images that are not directed by waking consciousness. For example, suppose a dream deals with the anxiety felt about embarking on a new venture. The dream may pull in our mother at the age she was on the day we started school for the first time. The scenery may be an alien landscape and we may find our dreaming self walking barefoot along a stony road. This dream would show us that what we feel today is similar to how we felt all those years ago. By addressing this we can understand why we feel anxious and also realize that we are no longer four years old and need not be so afraid of the world. Also, within the dream there will be clues as to how we can better manage our current anxiety. For instance, if we recognize why our unconscious produced a stony road for us to walk on, we can identify what the stones represent and take action in the present to smooth our road.

Emotional Climate Metaphors

Emotional climate metaphors are used all the time in our dreams and so it's important to take note of the climate, the environment or the weather conditions when you record your dream. A rainy day in a dream equates to a 'rainy day feeling' in our waking life, whereas a sunny day usually suggests we feel enthusiastic and optimistic. If, in waking life, a situation is getting out of control, we may dream of a hurricane or a tidal wave. If we're angry we may dream of a thunder storm or a wild fire. Bear in mind that these are generalizations. However, such common emotional climate metaphors do seem to be universally used in people's spoken language and in their dreams.

WHAT YOU'LL NEED

Paper & pen

INSTRUCTION

Step 1

Write your dream down in as much detail as you can remember, in the first person, present tense.

Step 2

Identify any residual feelings that stem from the dream. Read the dream out loud and take note of the feelings that are set in motion. Does the dream make you feel sad or anxious, or do you feel excited or uplifted as you read it?

Step 3

Try and link any aspect of the dream to some current event in your life. Freud referred to this as the *'day residue'*. It helps to establish a bridge between current preoccupations and the theme of the dream. It is often useful to write a detailed account of the previous day's events and thoughts.

Step 4

Use the Dream Association Technique to further elucidate the various elements in the dream. In that way, you will be gathering up some of the background thoughts that were translated into metaphor. When this process is combined with the identification of the 'day residue', it limits the range of applicable metaphors and helps to select the one that is most relevant to the dream and most compatible with your feelings and thoughts about the dream.

Step 5

The next step is to look at each scene in the dream as a metaphor, expressed in visual terms, and to speculate on the possible translation of this metaphor. At this point, don't be too concerned with the accuracy of the translation of the metaphor, concentrate more on the range of possibilities. If you're having trouble identifying the metaphors, remember that they will not necessarily be the common metaphors you are familiar with. For instance, I once dreamed of a girl whose face was covered in writing. She was whispering in my ear. I recognized this as a 'head full of words that need to be written down'. If it had been your dream, you may have seen a different metaphor. If the dream is long and complicated, work on what seems to be the most important metaphor first. This will narrow down the range of possible interpretations. Remember that the metaphors are portraying your perception of a situation and are, usually, represented in visual imagery, rather than in the dialogue that may occur within the dream. Once you've identified some of the metaphors, make a list of them and, alongside each one, write a few notes on how it relates to a current life situation.

Step 6

Write a brief synopsis of what you have discovered and how it relates to a real life situation. You can then judge whether it is appropriate to take any action. Often, seeing a life situation as a metaphor can give us a great deal of clarity and help us decide what we need to do to either change the situation or to manifest it in our future.

If you dream of this metaphor, your subconscious may be telling you to get more exercise!

14
DREAM MOCCASINS

The conscious ego can be a powerful censor that operates to maintain and support our (sometimes deluded) self-image. In Dream Moccasins you will rewrite the dream from the point of view of another dream character. You'll be amazed at how objectively you can view your own dream behavior. Are you acting like this, or would you like to act like this, in your everyday life?

WHAT YOU'LL NEED

Paper & pen

INSTRUCTION

Step 1
Identify a prominent character in the dream, this may be someone you know in reality or it may not. It does not even have to be another person; it can be anything in the dream that can be assigned an identity. Perhaps an animal, an item of furniture or even an ornament.

Step 2
Re-write the entire dream from this other character's perspective, both emotionally and spatially, and in the present tense. You need to spend some time getting into the character. Forget about how the 'dreaming you' felt in the dream. For instance, if your dream begins "I was riding a horse but couldn't control it. It started galloping and I nearly fell off." You may re-write it by beginning, "I'm a horse and the rider on my back keeps sticking her spurs into me. It hurts. I start to gallop in the hope that she'll fall off."

Step 3
Read the revised version of the dream through carefully. Immerse yourself in this new character. What can you conclude about the

actions, appearance or behavior of 'you' in the dream; the 'you' you are now observing rather than being?

Step 4
Does this remind you of anything that is happening or has happened in your life recently? If you're unsure of what the dream is about, use the Associative Technique to stimulate ideas connected to the dream symbols; this may shed more light on it.

Step 5
If the dream highlights a certain type of behavior on your part, think about what action you can take in your everyday life to change this behavior or address the issue or, perhaps, heal a difficult relationship.

Step 6
Having decided on the action you can take, resolve to DO IT.

15
DREAM MOSAIC

Using this method we aim to make a collage of photos, magazine clippings, drawings, words and anything else that you can find that appertains to your life, your hopes and any of your remembered dream images. Not only will it help elucidate your dreaming life, it will also inspire, motivate and encourage you to incorporate the dream messages into your waking life.

WHAT YOU'LL NEED

Lots of magazines containing color photographs and artwork.

Large sheet of paper, scissors and some glue.

INSTRUCTION

You don't need to have any particular dream in mind to start this project.

Step 1

Look through the material available and cut out anything that resonates either with your nighttime dreams or your waking reality. This may be photographs, drawings, text or anything else you can find. Anything goes.

Step 2

Once you're satisfied that you have enough material, and before you reach for the glue stick, arrange it all on the table in a way that it will fit onto your large sheet of paper. Take care doing this. Try and blend the separate things into a whole - how do they relate to each other? If you have a picture of a bear and another picture of a tree; perhaps your bear can be walking through the forest on his way to that beautiful house you'd love to live in one day. Arrange the clippings so that they overlap; we don't want any white paper showing underneath.

Step 3

Once you're happy with the arrangement, stick it all onto your paper in the same arrangement.

Step 4

If you've time, make up a storyboard of the events depicted in the mosaic so that they are all connected in a coherent tale.

Step 5

With your dream mosaic finished, place it in a location where you will see it often. Meditate on it every now and then and remember the messages of the dreams and how they relate to your life. Let it inspire and motivate you to bring the energy of the dream images into your waking reality.

The lady who made this mosaic is a 'cat person', with many feline attributes, who felt she needed the strength of bear to hold her family together. She was looking forward to a lifestyle change that would allow her to express her creativity.

16
DREAM RE-ENTRY

This is a very Shamanic way to work with your dreams as it is similar to a Shamanic journey. It gives tremendous insight into the dream and can also conjure up creative solutions or suggestions for action. A successful dream re-entry can be a startling experience, so be prepared! When done properly, it will connect you directly with whatever feelings, emotions or situations gave rise to the dream. It can also provide amazing insight into the creative power of your imagination. You don't have to work on a full dream, you can use this technique on a remembered fragment or even re-enter the dream specifically to speak with just one dream character. It's a useful technique for working on nightmares because it can be used to seek out and confront the dream object, or situation, that you found fearful. The technique will allow you to go back into the dream and ask questions of the thing you found frightening; ask it to explain why it was in your dream, what does it want from you? Instead of running away from it, as you may have done in your dream, you can stand your ground and ask it why it is chasing you. In this way, dream re-entry can be used to obtain a positive outcome.

For the technique to be successful, it's important that you're totally relaxed before you start. It also helps to have explored the dream beforehand so that you are absolutely familiar with the content.

WHAT YOU'LL NEED

Pen and paper or a Voice Recorder.

A bandana or something to cover your eyes.

A comfortable, warm, draught free place to lie down.

Relaxing music or Shamanic Drumming CD (optional).

Time - at least half an hour.

INSTRUCTION

Step 1
Write down the dream you are going to use in as much detail as possible, in the present tense. Read it over and over again before you start. Think about what it means. Have you any ideas? You might like to jot your ideas down so that you can compare them later with the experience.

Step 2
Get yourself into a comfortable position, preferably lying down. If you sit in a chair, make sure your head is supported. I've had some amazing re-entry journeys whilst relaxing in the bath, but if you do this make sure the water is going to stay hot for at least half an hour. Cover your eyes with a scarf or a bandana. For those new to the method, the re-entry can be done by guided visualization in a quiet environment. I've suggested a method for this at the end of these instructions. Those with experience in journeying may find a Shamanic drum or relaxing music more appropriate. Don't forget to switch off your phone!

Step 3
Do some deep breathing to make sure you're totally relaxed before you start. When you're ready, imagine yourself back in the dream at whatever point you feel is most appropriate. In the beginning you may find you have to control the direction of the dream to maintain focus. However, as the re-entry progresses you should find that it moved forward seemingly with its own autonomy. When this happens, behave just as you would in your everyday life. If you see a path, go and explore it. If you see an animal, actively engage with it and the dream characters you meet. Be aware of the environment, go exploring. Try and remember all details of the experience but don't do this at the expense of losing the experience. Often, we get so carried away with what's happening that we forget most of it. Providing you remember what seems to be the most important things, that will be enough. If you're using a Voice Recorder, you could try narrating your journey as

it's happening. If you can master this technique, it is the best way to do it as it will capture all of the detail.

Step 4

After the re-entry, make detailed notes of what transpired. If you used a Voice Recorder, play the recording back. Are there any new images or symbols present that weren't in the original dream? If there are, follow these up; find out more about them. This may involve going to your local library or doing a search of the World Wide Web. Do any new lines of thought occur to you as you do this? If so, jot them down. Be sure to carefully record any conversations you had with the characters you met.

Step 5

TAKE ACTION. Whatever you do, don't let all this powerful energy go to waste. If you've taken the trouble to do a re-entry on a dream, you must have felt the dream was important enough. A successful re-entry may not provide you with a full understanding of the meaning of the original dream but it, or the follow-up research, will always enable you to identify the life issue involved and suggest a solution or plan of action.

Step 6

Make a record of the outcome of the re-entry, and the action taken. I recommend you do this because often a re-entry acts like a scouting expedition where you accidentally bump into things from your future. It will also help you check whether the action taken has resulted in a positive outcome, especially if it wasn't necessarily the action you would have considered before the re-entry. This will not only be an interesting record for posterity but it will also reinforce, to your conscious mind, that you are taking your dreams seriously and honoring their messages. This, usually, results in enhanced dream recall and more entertaining and interesting dreams.

Guided Visualisation

You may want to record this on a Voice Recorder so that you are able to follow the instructions whilst you journey.

Imagine you're walking along a dirt path through a forest. Notice how the sunshine casts dappled, dancing shadows on the ground before you. You are barefoot and the soft ground feels good beneath your feet. Take a moment to concentrate on the feel of the soft, damp earth between your toes. .... Take a deep breath, fill your lungs with the fresh spring air. As you breathe in you are aware of the fresh scent of the trees and the carpet of bluebells and wild lavender. Enjoy their scent, breathe it into every part of your body. With every step you take, you feel more and more relaxed, all your cares and worries are a thousand miles away. Nothing can disturb this tranquil moment...................... As you walk on, you notice a huge old oak tree ahead of you. There's a figure standing by it. This is your dream messenger, the one who will lead you back into your dream. Study the figure closely so that you'll recognize them next time you meet. Your dream messenger greets you as you approach and slowly pushes open a heavy door set into the wide trunk of the oak tree. Disappearing into the gloom, your guide beckons you to follow. You step through the door and follow your dream messenger down a long flight of earthen steps. You feel perfectly safe knowing that no harm will befall you during this wonderful inner journey. There is nothing to be afraid of. Your guide tells you there are many steps to walk down, he suggests that you count them as you go down, starting with thirty and counting backwards..

You're now at the bottom of the steps and your dream messenger stops and stoops to open another door in front of you. You wait patiently in the dim light; the dank, dark air is somehow comforting.

Suddenly, the door swings open and your dream messenger invites you to step back into your dream.

17
DREAM SERIES

It can be argued that to take one dream in isolation is like examining the ear of an elephant whilst assuming it is the whole animal. If you're serious about exploring your own psychology through dream work, then looking for connections between your dreams is essential. It's thought that dreams occurring during the same sleep period, or over a few nights, often explore the same theme. This may not be apparent from a cursory examination of the dream material. Some dream researchers believe that dreams experienced at the beginning of the night relate to past experiences, brought into a dream to help us understand a current situation. Dreams in the middle of the night will incorporate images and experiences from the last couple of days and dreams just before waking contain the resolution or solution to the issue that initiated the first dream. This theory is based on the assumption that dreaming is a way of examining daily experiences to help us maintain and update our internal, emotional picture of ourselves and they do this by mixing old memory images with more recent ones. Your dreaming mind explores issues from many different angles; rehearsing all possible outcomes. So, although the issue under consideration remains the same, the stories that unfold can be dramatically different. If you look closely enough, you'll realize that there are always subtle connections, often difficult to recognize on a conscious level.

This technique is designed for multiple dreams occurring on the same night or over a short time period. However, you may recognize in your dream, an object, a person or a situation that you've dreamed of previously. Providing you've been keeping a dream journal, this technique can be used to good effect here.

A note on recurring dreams

Recurring dreams are those dreams that are dealing with long standing issues and so they often occur over extended periods of time. Often though, because the subconscious is working through the issue, it's only the theme that recurs rather than the actual dream content and so they are not always easy to spot. For instance; if I'm having trouble emotionally withdrawing from a past relationship, I may have dreams about bags, suitcases or hold-alls. Perhaps my dreaming self will try to pack too many things into a small suitcase, another time it might be struggling to carry too many bags, and yet another dream might find me discovering a bag I didn't know I had. All these scenarios can appear to be peripheral to the main action of the dream, perhaps because there are more pressing issues to address, like the row you had with your girlfriend yesterday because you're 'carrying too much baggage' around with you. In other words, the unconscious is more preoccupied with the effect this long standing issue is having on your life. The Dream Series Technique is an excellent method for exploring dreams such as these.

WHAT YOU'LL NEED

Lots of paper & a pen.

INSTRUCTION

Step 1
Write out each dream on a separate piece of A4 paper, using the first person, present tense. Include the date of the dream and, if possible, the time. Number them in the order they were dreamed.

Step 2
Give each dream a title that gives a flavor of the theme of the dream, in as few words as possible.

Step 3
Analyze all the dreams individually. If you have an unmanageable number, I suggest you limit yourself to six dreams initially. Make a note of your interpretation on the same sheet of paper as the dream itself. Bear in mind that this interpretation is not set in stone; you may find you need to modify it as you progress through this method and uncover more information.

Step 4

Explore Commonalities: Make a list of the symbols and characters in each of the dreams. Note any commonalities. Where a symbol or character appears in more than one of the dreams write this down in the centre of a new sheet of paper. Around this word place all the dream connections, making sure you include the number of the dream. Work outwards from these, adding all the thoughts, descriptions or associations you have with that unique symbol, like spokes radiating from a wheel hub. For example, if all the dreams have an element of escape or running away, you may find that what you are running away from is different in each dream. In this case, the centre of your hub may be, "Running Away", with the first layer of the spokes being, "Dream 1 Tiger, Dream 2 Monster, Dream 3 Husband." The next layer would be your personal associations to each of these symbols. Once completed, this diagram can be used to gain an in depth understanding of the elements within the dreams and the role they are currently playing in your life. If commonalities are not immediately apparent, look for elements that could link the dreams together. For instance; in one dream you may be returning a faulty item to a shop and in another be unable to remember where you parked your car after a shopping expedition. The common element here would be shopping and it is this that you would put into the centre of your diagram, with 'where's my car' and 'faulty goods' making the first layer of the spokes. It can also be very useful to use this method to explore all the helpful characters in the dreams to see what attributes and strengths they/you possess that can be used to your advantage. Do the same for any unhelpful characters, being aware that these are aspects of yourself that are hindering your progress.

Step 5

Synopsis: Write a brief synopsis of each dream, (the dream, not the interpretation).

Step 6

Translation and most salient point: Next, draw up a three column Table. In the first column, write the number assigned to the dream. Go through each synopsis and even more briefly translate it into a personal statement about yourself. For example; your synopsis might read, "I was in a Church at the funeral of a close friend. The Church was full and people were trying to stop the Priest from conducting the ceremony. It was very upsetting." Your translation may be something like; "A part of me, that I wanted to keep hold of, has died." Write this translation in the second column. It's important that you assume that all symbols, images and actions are aspects of yourself, in other words assume that your friend/sister/husband/wife/stranger is in the dream because of a character trait that you either have or that you need. Try and keep your notes as brief as possible, this will aid clarity and make the task more manageable. You can always go back and add more detail later.

Once you've done this, pick out the most salient emotion or action in each translation and enter this into the third column. Try and limit yourself to one word if you can. For example, in the illustration used above, the word that sums up the most salient point, might be "Death".

Look for a progression or advancement of ideas that indicates that your subconscious is working out how you can achieve your goal / resolve the problem. If the dreams remain essentially the same, without seeming to present any ideas for action, it could be an indication that there's a blockage somewhere and you may need to identify and deal with this before you can get a result.

Now write a Conclusion; a statement that you can easily remember, that embodies the overall message of the dream series.

Step 7
Merge the dreams: The next step requires you to be very creative and have some fun with your dreams. I want you to merge all the dreams into one but in such a way that they tell an empowering story. You can do this sequentially or you can overlay them. The nature of the dreams will dictate the best way to approach this. It isn't necessary to use all the detail from every dream and you can add tidbits of wisdom and insight that you've discovered along the way. You may find you have to write a

few drafts before you get a coherent merged dream. Imagine you're writing a synopsis of a block buster movie with you as the hero/heroine. This is a message from your inner Guru. Honour it. Let it empower you.

Step 8

ACTION: Make a list of all possible actions suggested by the dreams, no matter how bizarre some may seem at the moment. Exercise lateral thinking. And watch out for further dreams that seem to deal with the same issue. Are the dreams changing? If so, do they suggest a different course of action?

SYNOPSIS OF METHOD

Step 1   Write down each dream and allocate a number.

Step 2   Give each dream a title.

Step 3   Analyze each dream individually.

Step 4   Taking all dreams together, which elements are similar and which are contradictory? Do the elements that are similar show a progression of thought? If any elements are contradictory, can you relate them to your life?

Step 5   Write a brief synopsis of each dream.

Step 6   Translate each dream into a short, personal statement. Note down the most important point.

Step 7   Merge the dreams into one story.

Step 8   What action(s) is (are) suggested by the dreams?

18
DREAM SHIELD

The idea for this technique came from Henry Reed's book 'Getting Help From Your Dreams'. It's based on the Native American Medicine Wheel, which places the four directions (north, south, east, west) within a circle, each placed within one of four quadrants. Your finished shield will, in essence, be a mandala, which can be used as a personal meditation tool. There is a natural symmetry to the shield with opposed but balanced elements. The idea is to merge all the component parts into one picture. You can use one dream, or many with the same theme. This could be a life theme, or something you're currently considering. The finished shield should be imaginative and bring the lesson or message of the dream(s) into consciousness. With practice, the shield technique can be used to merge many different dreams together to form a story of your symbolic or spiritual life as a whole. It can even be an initiation into your own mythic quest.

I suggest that, initially, you use Carl Jung's *Psychological Functions* as your four quadrants:

a. Thinking opposite feeling (these deal with how we evaluate information and experiences).

b. Intuition opposite sensation (dealing with how we obtain information).

Jung believed that one of the functions is dominant over all the others at birth and that we must strive to develop the other three functions so that the four can operate as an harmonious whole. The function that's most difficult to develop is the one that's complimentary, or opposite, to the dominant function.

If you'd prefer not to use Jung's ideas, this technique can be applied to any psychological or spiritual belief system. Here are some ideas:

1. The four quadrants of the psyche can be interpreted in terms of the four sacred directions. For instance some belief systems see the East as the place of rebirth, others as the place of illumination. Choose whichever you're more familiar with. If

you don't follow any particular doctrine but want to use the idea of a medicine wheel, devise your own personal associations to the four directions.

2. Those readers who have knowledge of North American Shamanic practice will be familiar with the concept of the Medicine Wheel. Many indigenous North American tribes used it to make sense of the Universe. There are many variations in the interpretation of the four directions, what follows is the system used by the Plains Indians; the Cheyenne, the Crow and the Sioux. For more information about these tribes and how they used the concept of the medicine wheel, I would recommend that you read 'Seven Arrows' by Hyemeyohsts Storm, where you'll also find some beautiful illustrations of authentic medicine shields that will provide inspiration for your own work. These tribes believed that there are four great powers on the medicine wheel of life, North (representing wisdom, the color white and buffalo), South (representing innocence, the color green and mouse), East, (representing illumination, the color yellow and eagle), West, (representing introspection, the color black and bear). These four powers are gifts of perception, enabling us to live good lives in harmony with the earth and with each other. We are each born in one of the four quadrants and the power in that quadrant is dominant in our life. To become whole we must visit the other three directions and assimilate those gifts into our perception. Your Dream Shield can be a story map of your own visits to the four places of power.

3. The four quadrants can be representative of the four elements, earth (physical instincts), air (mind), fire (spirit) and water (emotion). Find symbols from your dreams that symbolize the activities of these four elements in your life. Do the four elements of your nature work together harmoniously, or are there instances when they're in conflict?

WHAT YOU'LL NEED

Pictures cut out of magazines, (optional)

Drawing materials including paints or colored pencils..

INSTRUCTION

Step 1

Find symbols from your dreams that reflect the activities of the four functions: thinking, feeling, sensation and intuition, or whatever system you have decided to use.

Step 2

Arrange these symbols into a coherent picture, keeping in mind where they need to be placed on the shield. There's no need to draw in the quadrants unless you want to, but you'll need to think about where their boundaries are within the shield. If you're using Jung's definitions, position the symbol of your dominant function at the top of the shield and its complimentary function at the bottom. Add whatever other dream symbols seem necessary to provide you with a sense of wholeness. If the symbols seem isolated from each other, add connectors. Try and achieve a balanced whole whilst remaining fully aware of the ideas, life experiences, thoughts and feelings that the symbols represent.

Step 3

Hang your shield on the wall where you can see it every day. You could even scan it and have it as the background on your desktop. Whatever you do with it, use it as a visual aid for meditation. Once its teachings are assimilated, you may be drawn to make another shield that honors your progress on your life's journey.

19

DREAM SOUND

Exploring the images in our dreams can sometimes lead to associations that are under the control of the ego. Sven Doehner, a Jungian Psychotherapist trained in Archetypal Psychology, believes he has found a way to eliminate this from dream working. He looks for the vibration or energy of the dream. This, he believes, will take us straight to the emotion that gave rise to it. This technique doesn't explore any of the sounds that may have been heard in the dream, instead we look to identify whereabouts in the body the dream resides and work on setting up a vibrational resonance between that area and the emotion of the dream. By describing the physical sensations and transforming them into a vocal sound, we can come to an experiential understanding of the emotion that caused the dream to occur. This method is not about cathartic release or primal screaming, it's about making a connection with the inner movement of energy; the energy that gave rise to the dream.

Sound can evoke unexpected reactions but it's the unexpected that causes changes in consciousness. Working with sound in this way, nurtures our relationship with the invisible and can transform those images that the ego is holding on to.

WHAT YOU'LL NEED

A group of people willing to push the boundaries of dream work.

INSTRUCTION

Step 1
The dreamer tells the dream to the group, taking care to express as fully as possible the emotion of the dream. Think about the smell, the taste, the feel of things within the dream and be aware of where the dream seems to reside within your body. Listeners must make careful mental note of how the person tells the dream. Listen to the subtleties, notice the body language, the expressions, the inflexions in the voice. Listen in

an experiential way. Concentrate on HOW the dream is being told rather than what's being said.

Step 2

Step back from the dream and identify the main theme or image. Individuals in the group suggest which scenes in the dream they think carry the most emotion. Many dreams contain a conflict and a turning point where things change. It's this turning point that is often the key to unlocking the emotion and revealing the essence of what's at risk at that moment. The dreamer listens to the suggestions and, with help from the facilitator, chooses one particular scene to work on. The dreamer will then retell that scene in detail.

Step 3

The dreamer, with the help of the group, then tries to identify the core emotion or theme and the place it resides inside their body. Decide on a one word concept and then turn it into a phrase that captures the essence of the conflict/the turning. Individuals in the group are encouraged to suggest appropriate phrases, which should be stated in the first person, present tense. The phrases are stated out loud and the dreamer must decide which she wants to work with. An example of phrases that might be suggested; 'It's not my fault', 'I'm the last one remaining', 'I watch it go'. The chosen phrase is repeated a number of times so that the dreamer can hear it stated clearly; this is called mirroring. The facilitator will repeat the chosen phrase out loud with different intonations and emotions, for example; sadness, anger, frustration, scorn, dower, seductive, questioning, convincing, apologetic, sincerely. The facilitator must watch closely the reaction of the dreamer to each intonation as a marked reaction to one will help guide the dreamer to the correct sound.

Step 4

The dreamer must now go inside themselves and concentrate on where the emotion is residing in their body. With practice they will begin to feel a vibration in that place. They must now make a sound that synchronizes the vibration until they feel the sound vibrating in their body where the emotion resides. We're not looking for melody. We're looking to achieve resonance between the sound and the inner vibration; a sound expression beyond the ego. Play with the initial sound until it becomes a true reflection of the part of the dream being worked on. You should spend at least ten minutes doing this. The sound we start with will not be the sound we end up with; find a blend. Don't rush it. If the dreamer needs support or help, tuning forks A and D can help to refine the sound. When the dreamer feels they have got the correct sound, ask them to make the same sound but clearer, louder. They must open their mouth and their throat, and keep their head straight. This isn't about forcing oneself to make a sound, we just want the sound to appear and then fine tune it to what was felt inside.

Step 5

The dreamer will know when they have achieved the pure sound. There will be no effort involved, it will just come up from the depths of their being. They must make this pure sound at least three times, exhaling completely at the end of each one. This awakens the transcendence function and produces a unique personal mantra. Don't be surprised if some members of the group begin to cry at this point. These primal sounds can elicit powerful feelings of empathy.

Step 6

The listeners now describe the sound they heard in terms of feelings/emotions, commenting on any inflexions and any changes they felt in their own physiology. Attention should be paid to the dreamer at all times. Producing sound from out of the depths of our being is a very emotional experience that can release a lot of tension. To protect the dreamer, close your eyes when addressing any vulnerable points. The dreamer's reactions to what's being said is invaluable information and can be fed back to them before the session closes.

Step 7

This process cannot be rushed, it will take as long as it takes.

Step 8

It's important to close this session with delicacy and compassion towards both the dreamer and the group as a whole. It often helps to hold the session in sacred space with candles in the centre of the circle. The candles can then be extinguished at the end as a sign of closure.

20
DREAM THEATRE

Re-enacting your dream is a powerful way to experience its energy and understand its message. It's not a technique that can be used alone as its success lies in the fact that other people make the dream come alive by role-playing your dream characters for you. Drama and theatre are very healing, therapeutic tools and so this technique works well with dreams that left the dreamer with an uneasy feeling.

WHAT YOU'LL NEED

A group of people and any props that are to hand.

INSTRUCTION

Step1

Choose a dream that's relatively short with a maximum of six living characters. The dreamer tells the dream to the group, describing any emotions he/she experienced during the dream.

Step 2

The dreamer then chooses people from the group to play the different characters and also the props if appropriate. For instance, a house can be a group of people standing in a square. One person can be the door, another can be a table etc.... Be inventive. Be creative. Have fun. The dreamer will play themselves as they were in the dream.

Step 3

The dreamer must issue brief instructions to the actors, in terms of stage directions only, they must not give advice on how the part should be acted. Although the dreamer is in charge throughout the re-enactment, he must allow the participants to express the energy of their character in whatever way they feel is appropriate. It may be necessary to run through the dream a number of times, until the dreamer feels the energy is right. Remember this does not have to be a serious business;

87

the more fun you have, the more positive will be the outcome. However, if the dreamer feels a somber re-enactment is more appropriate, then that is how things should proceed. The dreamer is in control throughout.

Step 4

When the re-enactment has come to a satisfactory conclusion, the dreamer may then ask all the participants how they felt acting out the role assigned to them. Much information can be gleaned from this, often shedding new light on the dream.

Step 5

The dreamer is now free to discuss the dream meaning with the group in the fashion of Montague Ullman's 'If this were my dream' if he/she so wishes. There should be no obligation to do this. The dreamer must then decide, with the help of the group, how the dream may be changed to obtain a more positive outcome. For instance, the dream may have ended in a car crash. The dreamer may now want to drive her car in a different direction, at a different time. Or indeed, choose a different driver or go by bus.

Step 6

The group then re-enact the changed dream.

Step 7

To close the session, the dreamer can thank the group and share any thoughts or insights he/she may have had about the dream or the process.

21
DREAM THEME

The Dream Theme method aims to identify the life issue or situation that gave rise to the dream by identifying its theme. This may be a major life issue, or may simply be expressing personal characteristics, attitudes or behavior. Intensive work on a dream theme can give you a better understanding, not only of the personal meaning of a dream and what is important to you at the time, but also of yourself and how you react to certain situations in your life. You will also have the opportunity to identify a desired outcome, which can be consciously acted upon in your daily life. Doing this can result in profound changes; changes that may not previously have been considered.

If you record your dreams over a period of time, you will often find that the same theme is repeated in different dreams at different times. If you examine these dreams using this method and are able to relate them to events going on in your life at the time, you may well discover the life situation or emotion that causes them to occur. You'll also find that the dreams will change over time, showing how you are adapting to and integrating the life issue under scrutiny. This can be a valuable life lesson.

WHAT YOU'LL NEED

Paper & pen

INSTRUCTION

Step 1
Write the dream down in as much detail as you can, in first person, present tense.

Step 2
Identify the Theme of the dream. Often, you will be able to discover this by asking yourself what is the main energy of the dream; what are

you, as the dream character, physically doing and who or what are you doing this with/to? It's useful to take away all the detail from the dream, e.g. names, things, places etc… and leave only the action. This should leave you with a clear theme. This is perhaps the most difficult step, so don't worry if you can't decide what the theme is from the outset. Once you've gone through Steps 3 and 4, the theme will often become clear.

Step 3

Ask yourself how the "dreaming you" was affected by the events in the dream. Did you run away for instance, or did it just make you feel angry, hurt, frightened? Again, try and write as briefly as possible. Now try and match the Theme, and how the dream events affected you, to a specific area of your life The symbols, images and environment of the dream may provide useful clues to this, but take care not to be distracted from the main task.

Step 4

Now write down any questions that the dream prompts you to ask of yourself or the dream character(s). For instance, why did I run away? If this dream had been a real life event, would I have reacted in the same way? Attempt to answer these questions on a conscious level, taking care to relate the issues to events occurring in your life.

Step 5

Finally, decide on an outcome. What do you need to do (or think) in order to resolve the issue raised in the dream? Do you need to modify your behavior towards, or your reaction to, the dream event? Is there some action you can take to make the situation better. Or perhaps you need to stop doing something you're currently doing. Depending on the nature of the dream you may want to adapt this method slightly. For instance, in observer dreams it may be more appropriate to describe how a certain action affected the main character, rather than you as the dreamer. If you do this, you must nevertheless assume that this dream character represents yourself.

22
EXPERIENTIAL DREAM WORKING

This is a method for going straight to the heart of a dream and experiencing its message without getting involved in difficult analyses or interpretation. It was proposed by Alvin Mahrer in his book 'Psychotherapy and Self-change'. It's similar to both the Gestalt technique and Dream Re-entry but differs from the former by focusing on only one dream character, i.e. the character having the emotional experience. Like Gestalt, however, this method assumes that all characters are projections of the self.

It differs from Dream Re-entry by only focusing on an identifiable "peak moment". The secret of success with this technique is in the identification of the peak moment.

WHAT YOU'LL NEED

A Voice Recorder.

INSTRUCTION

Step 1

Choose a dream and recount a few recent life situations that the dream calls to mind. Try and identify the moment of peak feeling in the real life situation(s). Don't spend too long doing this. If nothing springs to mind in the first ten minutes, move on. This step can often be done after the 'dream experiencing'.

Step 2

Sit quietly in a relaxed position and recall the dream in as much detail as you can. Identify the peak feeling(s) in the dream and clarify what is happening during these moments. Focus your attention on what you are feeling and the point in the dream at which this feeling is strongest. For example; do you feel fear? If so, what's frightening you? If you're being chased, think about who or what is chasing you and try and identify the exact point in the dream at which the fear peaks. For instance; "Suddenly I can see my pursuer's face; he's wearing a mask, it's terrifying." In this case, the appearance of the mask, rather than the feeling of being pursued, would be the peak moment.

Step 3

Now switch on the Voice Recorder and enter into that peak moment fully, living and existing in it as if it were really happening, all the while speaking out loud about what you are experiencing. Imagine you're re-living a real experience. Remember, you're not looking for anymore than what is happening in the dream at the moment of peak feeling so it's important not to let your mind wander. If you've identified more than one peak moment in the same dream you must repeat the process for the second peak.

Step 4

Play back the recording and, as you listen, think about what's being said in the context of the dream as a whole. Do any situations in the past spring to mind as you do this? These situations may be very remote, perhaps even events (or seemingly non-events) that occurred in your childhood. If the peak moment is joyful or happy you will often be looking for a remote situation where the dream experiencing could or should have occurred, but didn't.

Step 5

Now apply the experiencing within the context of recent real life situations. Imagine yourself behaving in a recent life event in the same way. How do you feel about that? Could you have done things differently?

Step 6

Think about how you can apply this experiencing to your life. This may be in the form of behavioral changes or a different way of looking at something. Doing this will often highlight real possibilities for the future or serve as a springboard for focused action in the present.

23
FIVE STAR METHOD

This technique, devised by G. Scott Sparrow, is a dream work approach based on a co-creative view of dreaming. The theory of co-creation, a term first used by Ernest Rossi, is based on the idea that the dream is an unfolding relationship between the dreamer and the dream content, rather than being derived from a single source (e.g. the unconscious). This means that, throughout the dream, we are making decisions about what comes next based on what has just happened in the dream story. It takes the focus away from the dream story per se and shifts it onto why the dream story progressed as it did.

So rather than looking for the message within the dream, this method gives an opportunity to explore the decision making that occurred whilst the dream was in progress. It's based on the premise that when we enter the dream state, we become aware of, and often challenged by, unacknowledged or rejected aspects of ourselves. Our attempts to deal with, or avoid, these issues during the dream greatly affects the resultant dream experience. The method is best used on a one to one basis. The instructions that follow are based on this model.

WHAT YOU'LL NEED

Paper & pen

INSTRUCTION

Step 1: Share dream and feelings
Dreamer shares the dream in the first-person, present tense. Listener identifies with the dreamer's experience, and shares feelings that may arise. Dreamer also shares feelings provoked by the dream.

Step 2: Formulate the theme
In collaboration with the Dreamer, the Listener summarizes the action in the form of a succinct theme. Avoid mention of specific images and names. Use generic nouns like "someone," "something," or

"somewhere" to replace specifics names, objects and places. Example: "Someone is trying to get somewhere, and encounters an array of obstacles blocking their way."

Step 3: Highlight and troubleshoot Dreamer responses

In collaboration with the Dreamer, the Listener highlights and troubleshoots the Dreamer's responses to the dream content. Highlight the responses (i.e. assumptions and reactions) that were made by the Dreamer. Ask, "Where did you respond or react to the dream situations and characters?" Follow up with questions such as, "Do you respond this way in other areas of your life?" "Is this a new response, or is it familiar?" Try and tease out what was constructive about the Dreamer's responses. What was unfortunate about the Dreamer's responses? Ask the Dreamer if they think they could have responded differently, and what they think would have happened if they had.

Step 4: Analyze the imagery

The Dreamer shares his or her associations with the images. The Listener can also share their own associations and ideas, provided they make it clear these are their own projections. As an added step, have the Dreamer dialogue (role play) with dream images in order to enhance awareness and deepen the relationship with that part of himself/herself. The goal is to clarify the generic issue or unconscious agenda represented by the dream content. Also, the Listener and Dreamer can discuss any changes that may have occurred in the dream images in the course of the dream, and why those changes may have occurred.

Step 5: Apply the dream

Ask the Dreamer, "If you had this dream again, what would you like to do differently? How do you think that would affect the outcome?" Also ask, "Where else in your life can this new response be helpful? Where are you willing to enact this new response?" Following this dialogue, the Dreamer should make detailed notes of what they have learned and any follow-up action they may wish to take.

24

GESTALT TECHNIQUE

The German word *gestalt* means whole or complete. Fritz Perls **(1893-1970)** developed Gestalt therapy because he wanted to make dream work easy to understand and available to everyone.

The gestalt technique assumes that all dream characters and images are aspects of ourselves. This is not an assumption that all dream workers make but for this method, it is a prerequisite. Even if you don't agree with it, I would urge you to experiment with it as it's a good method to employ before exploring other avenues, especially if the there seems to be some conflict in the dream. Sometimes we deny uncomfortable thoughts or emotions and this can result in these things being displaced or polarized in our waking life. Such inner conflicts show up in dreams as opposites, disagreements or differences of opinion, often portrayed as arguments or fights. By realizing that the "other person" in your dream, who seems to be outside of yourself, is actually a part of you, enables you to begin to explore those feelings that you may have disowned. Acknowledging them, and trying to understand where they come from, will allow you to take them back inside of yourself and assimilate them. Gestalt is also a powerful method to use if you're experiencing disputes in your waking life. It can help you understand the reason behind the behavior and actions of other people.

As well as working on the characters in our dreams, we can also use this technique on inanimate objects such as vases, chairs, trees. By way of a brief explanation, imagine you've had a dream about a tree. This tree will not be a *real* tree nor will it be just any old tree. We will not find this particular tree in dream dictionaries. The only way to learn about this tree is to experience it, watch it, see how it behaves, *become the tree* and speak with the voice of the tree. Its leaves, its branches, the way it moves in the wind, is a complete statement within itself. This goes for everything in the dream, whether it be a person, an animal, a plant or something as inane as a vase.

WHAT YOU'LL NEED

Labeled chairs.

Pen and paper

Voice Recorder (optional).

INSTRUCTION

Step 1

Having chosen a dream to work on, pick out the main characters or symbols (as many as you wish) and write out a label for each one. For example; man with stick, woman with fair hair, dog etc... Arrange some chairs or cushions in a circle; one place for each character/symbol. If you're working with a partner, they can make notes of what you say though it is possible to use this method successfully when working alone. In either case, it is helpful to record what you say on a Voice Recorder, this way nothing is missed.

Step 2

Sit in the chair that represents yourself. If you were just an observer in the dream then you should sit in a chair labeled "observer". Start off by retelling the dream in the **first** person and **present** tense. Having done this, move from one chair to another playing the role of each character or symbol. Begin by expressing the character's viewpoint, then ask questions of other characters/images. For instance; imagine that in the dream you're dragging a dog round on a lead. As the dog, you may say you feel tired all the time and have no energy. You may want to ask "you" why you are being so cruel. "You" (as yourself) may reply that you are fed up with the dog who you think is lazy and won't walk anywhere. You must sit in the chair of whichever character you are playing and it's a good idea to spend a few moments "getting into the character" before you begin to speak. If working with a partner, they should remain silent and refrain from asking you questions or commenting on your role play.

Step 3

When you've exhausted the dream characters, sit down quietly and write a brief synopsis of each one. If you've done the exercise with a partner, they should be able to provide some useful input at this stage. Try and identify in what area of your life you are behaving or feeling like each of the characters. Are any of the characters in conflict with each other? If so, you can be sure that this is highlighting a problem you have in your waking life. If the conflict involves a dream character who is known to you, try and be objective and act as if the person is an aspect of you rather than them playing themselves. Are you behaving that way to someone else? This step requires us to try and be honest with ourselves and this is why it's useful to work with a partner. Others often see us much more honestly and clearly than we see ourselves. Be prepared to listen and ponder!

Step 4

Decide what the dream is telling you. Is it highlighting a situation past or present? Is it dealing with a relationship issue? If so, with whom? Is there any way in which you can now change your behavior or beliefs to make improvements in your everyday life?

Step 5

Decide if you need to take any action. If so, DO IT.

25

GO WITH THE FLOW

This method will appeal to those who prefer a more organized approach to dream analysis. The dream is dissected in an analytically linear fashion, which encourages clear thought processes about each event occurring in a dream. However, it is open to abuse by the ego censorship so be vigilant. Despite this, it is a useful technique to use in order to decide whether or not to subject a particular dream, or dream image, to a more thorough analysis.

WHAT YOU'LL NEED

A large sheet of paper and lots of different colored pens.

INSTRUCTION

Step 1

Begin by splitting the dream into a sequence of significant events. Write the events in a row across the top of the paper, enclosing each event in its own 'bubble', (see the illustration at the end of the instructions).

Step 2

In a row below, ask two questions of each event. For instance, if the dreaming you was walking along a path, you may want to ask, "Where did I think the path was leading?" and, "What was the path like under foot?" Or perhaps you were in an argument with another dream character and want to ask, "Why did she yell at me?" or "Why was she wearing a blue cardigan?" Join the event to the questions by arrows.

Step 3

In a row below, give answers or responses to each question. It's always a good idea to write down your first thought about this rather than spend time deliberating over what you think the answer should be.

Step 4

Reflect on what you have written so far. You might want to make notes of things that occur to you on a separate piece of paper. If things from the past come to mind, it's very important to try and relate these to the present.

Step 5

What conclusions can you make about the dream events? How are they related? Pay particular attention to the sequence. The second event happened because of the first event; think in terms of cause and effect. What was it about the first event that prompted your dreaming mind to conjure up the second event and so on? What was the dream about do you think? How does it relate to your present circumstances?

Step 6

Is there any action you could take to resolve or drive forward the issue raised in the dream? If the dream has highlighted a particular problem, what could you do to resolve the problem? Perhaps the dream was about a hope or ambition for the future? If so, does the dream suggest anything you could do to help make this a reality? Whatever action springs to mind, if it feels right, DO IT!

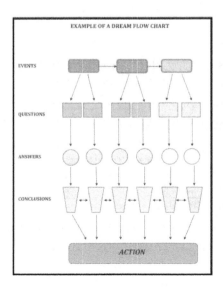

26
HAIKU DREAMING

Haiku is a fixed form of poetry that originated in Japan over 300 years ago. It's a short set of words that expresses the essence of a unique thought, moment or feeling. The structure of Haiku can be used as a framework for understanding and expressing a dream in a way that is focused only on the main message of the dream. A Haiku consists of three lines of: 5, 7, 5 syllables respectively and the aim of this technique is to condense your dream into this format.

It's a great technique to use in a dream sharing group, especially if participants are asked beforehand to bring along a Haiku poem they have already prepared. At the beginning of the session, participants are invited to read their Haiku aloud. The group can then decide which dream they will work on.

WHAT YOU'LL NEED

Paper & pen.

INSTRUCTION

There are three applications for Haiku in Dream Work. Use whichever fits your dream best.

Method 1

Develop and expand a single dream image or symbol into a full expression of its meaning. This involves playing around with the words in your dream report. Add whatever new words and associations come to mind. How does this image make you feel? Can you identify any metaphors in the dream story? Look at the dream in terms of its symbolic meaning, what is it representing? If it could speak to you, what would it say? Does it remind you of something in the past? Condense all this information into a few words and fit these words into the constraints of the Haiku.

Example:

Brown bear is scary.
He's strong and fearsome and tall.
Not like my teddy.

Method 2

Condense an entire dream. This type of condensation is particularly helpful in a dream group where there are time constraints and yet you want to make sure that everyone gets a chance to participate. Perhaps spend a few minutes at the beginning of the session for each person to prepare a Haiku version of the dream they've brought to the group. Each person reads their Haiku out loud followed by a moment of silence to allow the dream to touch everyone and to allow reactions. The haiku reveals the heart of the matter and thus quickly promotes fruitful discussion.

Example:

Sick on a journey.
Stumbling over parched fields.
My dream wanders on.

Method 3

Here we superimpose the dream onto our waking reality, giving us an insight into how the dream relates to our life. Begin by condensing the essence of the dream into the first two lines of the haiku. Use the third line to convey some truth about your life that correlates with the dream vision.

Example:

Angry dancing girl.
Asks why I'm looking at her.
She thinks she's not loved.

27
LIGHTNING DREAMWORK

This technique was developed by Robert Moss as a way to share dreams on a daily basis. As the name implies, it's a quick method that can be used anywhere at any time, even with total strangers. Robert believes that, as a society, we have lost the art of telling our dreams in a way that holds the listeners attention. We often mix up the story, get confused, back track, or add little snippets of background information. This causes the dream to lose its power and often the listener will respond by voicing their own views about what the dream means, or ask questions that violate the dreamer's privacy.

The Lightning Dreamwork process makes it possible to share dreams in such a way that they retain their primal energy and magic. It also encourages useful, objective feedback from the listener.

WHAT YOU'LL NEED

You won't need anything for this method except a willing partner.

INSTRUCTION

Step 1: Telling the dream as a story with a title
The dreamer starts by giving their dream a title. They then tell (not read) the dream as simply and clearly as possible. Leave out autobiography, and tell the dream as a story, complete in itself. When you do this, you claim your power as a storyteller and communicator.

Step 2: The partner asks the 3 vital questions
Question 1: How did you feel when you woke up?
The dreamer's first emotional reactions to the dream are vital guidance on the basic quality of the dream and its relative urgency.

Question 2: Reality check
The reality check question is designed to establish whether the dream reflects situations in waking life, including things that might

manifest in the future. Dreams often contain guidance about the possible future, and it's important not to miss these messages. By running a reality check, we help to clarify whether a dream is primarily (a) literal (b) symbolic, or (c) an experience in a separate reality.

In practice, the partner may need to ask several specific reality check questions focusing on specific elements in the dream. Here are a couple that can be applied to just about any dream:

Do you recognize any of the people or elements in the dream in waking life?
Or
Could any of the events in this dream possibly happen in the future?

Question 3: *What would you like to know about this dream?*

This simple question to the dreamer provides a clear focus for the next step.

Step 3: "If it were my dream"

Next the partner tells the dreamer, "If it were my dream, I would think about such-and-such." It's very important that the ethical protocol discussed in the chapter 'Sharing Your Dreams' is followed.

As the partner, you can bring in any associations, feelings or memories that the dream arouses in you, including dreams of your own that may contain similar themes. You must not presume that you know what their dream means. All you can do is say what it would mean for you, if it were your dream. This means your comments must be relevant to your life and not to the life of the dreamer.

Step 4: Taking action to honor the dream

Finally the partner says to the dreamer,
How are you going to honor this dream or act on the guidance it gives?
Acting on your dream brings the magic of a deeper reality into your waking life. One of the actions you can take is to write a personal motto that sums up the dream message. This can be hung on your wall, or used as a bumper sticker on your car. Look at it every day so you are constantly reminded of the energy of the dream and the call to action.

28
ONCE UPON A TIME THERE WAS A DREAM

The idea for this technique came from the book by Jill Mellick, 'The Art of Dreaming'.

Fairy Tales deal with archetypal situations that are as old as humanity. They also speak in the language of the universal unconscious and this is why they have endured and stayed popular through countless generations. Many dreams contain archetypal images and stories, especially those dreams described by Carl Jung as 'big dreams'. If you have such a dream, brilliant! If not, choose a dream that has an interesting story line. You may find, after doing this exercise, that the dream does deal with archetypal issues after all.

WHAT YOU'LL NEED

Paper & pen.

A dream containing an archetypal character or theme if possible.

INSTRUCTION

This exercise seems to work better if you put yourself under a little pressure. So, give yourself twenty minutes to complete your story. It doesn't have to be perfect; at this stage the flow is more important than the 'thinking'. Here are a few points for you to follow:

1. Begin with the line, 'Once upon a time...' and write in the past, i.e.: 'there was a, she went to . . . etc'.

2. Exaggerate as much as you can. Make small things very tiny, and big things enormous.

3. Use as many adjectives as possible, (yes I know this is banned in literary fiction!)

4. Give a name to every important element, and describe how it looks, feels, smells etc...

5. Use the words 'always' 'ever' and 'never' as much as you can

6. Use all the senses

7. Make use of dialogue (very helpful to create a 'turning point')

8. Create a happy ending, e.g. 'and they lived happily ever after'.

9. Give the story a title that will intrigue a six year old child

Here's an example of how a story might begin:

Once upon a time there was a beautiful Princess who smelled as sweet as lavender. One day, as she played in the arboretum, that was called Heaven on Earth, she thought about how blessed her life was. There could not be a happier Princess in the whole of Fairy Tale Land. Everything was perfect. As she mused and twiddled her golden locks around her fingers, a man entered through the gate at the far end of the garden; where the holly bushes danced with the oak tree. It was her Prince, or so she thought, and she waved gleefully in greeting. But as he came closer, she saw that he was a wolf man with a long snout and sharp, black eyes. He was holding something shiny and metallic and it caused the sun to cast flickers of light that danced on his face. Bang! A gunshot echoed inside her head. The red roses trembled around her and their petals fell to the ground like drops of blood.

"What have you done?" she cried.

"I've broken your heart into pieces." Wolf man replied.

29
POSTCARD FROM A DREAM

Write a message to send to someone or something in your dream. Write the message on a postcard and draw or paint a picture on the front. Your message could be a request for further communication or assistance, or merely a thank you for being in your dream. Be creative!

WHAT YOU'LL NEED

Paper & pen & artist materials.

Blank Postcards

If doing group work, supply a selection of postcards to use as examples.

INSTRUCTION

Step 1

Choose a dream that has an identifiable character that you can recognize; it may be someone in your life, past or present, or may be an aspect of yourself. It may not be a person at all, it could be an animal or even an inanimate object.

Step 2

Take a blank postcard and draw a picture of your dream, or the dream character, on the front.

Step 3

Given the dream story, what message would you want to send to this person/character? Write it on the postcard.

Step 4

It's quite fun to address the postcard to your home address, stick a stamp on and post it. When it drops into your letter box, you'll be reminded of the dream and its message.

For example:

I might dream of a bear and, in my dream, be afraid and try to run away. I may consciously recognize, however, that I need the strength of bear to get me through a current crisis. My postcard may, therefore, be a picture of a bear, with the message: "I'm sorry I ran away. Please meet me in the dreamtime tonight." The example below is from a dreamer who was procrastinating about moving house. She recognized that the part of her that was driving the dream car, was the part that could make a decision and get things moving.

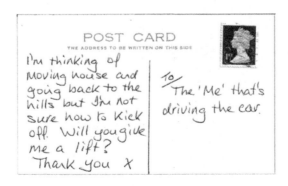

30
TRANSFORMATIONAL DREAMS

How we relate to other people is of paramount importance, not only to our psychological health, but also to society as a whole. We are social creatures so it's not surprising that many of our dreams are concerned with relationships. Perhaps dreams are a way of integrating and assimilating our knowledge of others in order that we may have more productive social interaction. It's a sad fact that, so often, relationship difficulties are caused when other people don't behave in the way we think they should. We have expectations of them and when those expectations are not met, we find ourselves unhappy or in conflict. Sometimes we demand that the other person changes rather than us taking responsibility for the way that we have reacted. Sometimes we just don't consider that it may be us that needs to change. Undoubtedly, some dreams suggest that we are reacting to a current situation in the same way we reacted to a similar situation in the past. Same story, but different props. If this reaction caused problems last time, then it's likely to be causing problems in the present as well. This is why dreams touch on past events and emotions and mix them up with things going on in the present. It's as if the dream is saying, "Here we go again, watch out!" or "Something very similar has happened before, let's try a different outcome".

If appropriate, this technique gives the opportunity to transform difficult relationships into something more positive by considering changing our behavior, or our reaction, rather than expecting the other person to change or meet our expectations. This technique, however, doesn't guarantee that troublesome relationships can always be healed. Sometimes a positive outcome may be that you discover you need to walk away and stop beating yourself up about a relationship that is detrimental to your well being.

WHAT YOU'LL NEED

A current dream, plenty of time and lots of courage.

INSTRUCTION

Step 1

Choose a dream that appears to be about your relationship with another person. Write out your dream in as much detail as you can remember.

Step 2

Try and connect your dream to current events and circumstances. This is an important step as it provides a focus, especially if the dream seems rather bizarre and confused. Don't just look for connections in the same day, in my experience occurrences in daily life are often not reflected in dreams for two or three days. So bear this in mind when you are looking for what Freud called "day residue". Also think about what was on your mind during the day before the dream? Did you go to sleep mulling over a particular problem or thinking about something or someone?

Step 3

Give the dream a title; this will help you identify the underlying theme.

Step 4

Look closely at the symbols or images in the dream. What are your personal experiences or associations to these images? What about the dream characters? Are they people known to you or strangers? Where did the dream take place? What are your associations with this environment?

Step 5

Look at the action of the dream. What was going on? Who was doing what to whom and why? Can you relate this to your life in the present or in the past?

Step 6

Explore the emotions you felt in the dream and compare these to the emotions you are feeling now as you think about the dream. How did you feel about the characters in your dream; their appearance or behavior? How do you feel about their behavior now as you remember the dream? Have you had other dreams about this character? Is there any area of your life where you feel as you did in the dream?

Step 7

Spend time meditating on the dream and what you have discovered so far. Does the dream reflect current effects from past or recent experiences with the person featured in the dream or some other person? If it reminds you of a situation with someone in your life; who is this someone? How are they similar to the dream character? What is the state of your relationship with them? Could it be improved? What could you do to transform the relationship? If you did in reality whatever it was you did, or didn't do, in the dream, what do you think would happen?

Step 7

Does your dream suggest some action? This may be an integral part of the dream or may just be something that occurs to you as you reflect on the dream. It may just be a change of mind, attitude or behavior. After careful consideration, decide on the action you will take. It may be as simple as telephoning the person just to say 'Hi' or as big as a major shift in your relationship with them. Remember, talking is good. Talking can resolve problems. If you decide that a confrontation is necessary to clear the air, a good starting point is to tell them your dream. Discuss it with them. How do they feel about your dream? Invite them to comment on what they would think it meant if they'd had the dream.

Afterword

Exploring a relationship, using this technique, will highlight all positive and negative aspects of that relationship. If anything negative is highlighted I suggest you pay attention to dreams occurring in the next few days or weeks and work on those dreams in the same way. After careful consideration, if you feel the negative aspects of the relationship are causing you harm, emotionally, spiritually or physically, revisit the dreams and see whether they suggest a way through. Sometimes the only way through is a way out. If this is what you decide, look to your dreams. They can give you the courage to walk away.

Believe in your dreams, believe in yourself.

APPENDIX I: WHEN TO USE THE TECHNIQUES

TECHNIQUE	Working alone	One-2-one	Group work
A Good Story: Plot Analysis	✓	✓	
Associative Technique	✓	✓	
Book of the Dream	✓		
Box of Dreams	✓	✓	
Double D - Doing & Describing	✓	✓	
Dream Animals	✓	✓	✓
Dream Detective		✓	✓
Dream Drawing Story Game		✓	✓
Dream Duals	✓		
Dream Fiction	✓		
Dream Gift	✓		✓
Dream Mapping	✓		
Dream Metaphors	✓	✓	
Dream Moccasins	✓	✓	
Dream Mosaic	✓		✓
Dream Re-entry	✓		✓
Dream Series	✓		
Dream Shield	✓		✓
Dream Sound			✓
Dream Theatre			✓
Dream Theme	✓	✓	
Experiential Dream Working	✓	✓	
Five Star Method		✓	
Gestalt Technique	✓	✓	✓
Go With The Flow	✓		
Haiku Dreaming	✓		✓
Lightning Dream Work		✓	✓
Once Upon A Time	✓	✓	✓
Postcard From A Dream	✓		✓
Transformational Dreams	✓		

APPENDIX II: LESSON PLANS FOR KS2 *

Sleep and Dreaming

The topic is covered over two sessions, the first on 'Sleep' and scheduled to take forty five minutes and the second, on 'Dreaming' scheduled for one hour. The Lesson Plans and accompanying Questionnaires are reproduced here. Please feel free to use these resources, all I ask is that you reference the source.

At the sessions, students are given the 'Sleeping & Dreaming Questionnaire'. The information contained therein is referred to throughout the sessions.

In the first Lesson Plan, reference is made to 'Laminated Data Boards'. These are highly visual boards that I produced for data collection. They are optional but if you've time to prepare them, they will add interest and engage the children more fully in the proceedings. They contained illustrations of whatever was being voted on, alongside a large box in which to enter five bar gates as a method of counting votes. Students entered their vote on the board themselves.

Following these sessions, many of the children started writing their dreams down and bringing them into school to share.

* **Key Stage 2** is a UK legal term for the four years of schooling in maintained schools in England and Wales normally known as Year 3, Year 4, Year 5 and Year 6, when pupils are aged between 7 and 11.

LEARNING OUTCOMES

LESSON 1: Sleep

1. Pupils will develop their own ideas about why we sleep.

2. They will begin to understand that science doesn't always have an answer – they will learn the difference between hypothesis and theory, and the fact that hypotheses are often hotly disputed.

3. They will review their own sleep pattern and needs.

4. They will think about the position they sleep in – does everyone sleep in this position? They will experiment with different body positions and report on the physical and emotional effects of lying in different positions.

5. They will hear about body clocks (circadian rhythms) and think about how their own body clock affects them

6. They will accumulate data that can later be used to produce graphs and charts

LESSON 2: Dreaming

1. Pupils will think about why they dream and what they dream about.

2. By recognising they dream of things not in their everyday life, they will begin to think about symbolism and imagination.

3. They will discover that other children dream of the same things.

4. They will be introduced to the fact that all animals are thought to dream – evidenced by REM.

5. Children will choose their own media for expressing one of their own dreams (or someone else's) – painting, drawing, writing or making a collage.

6. They will also hear about famous painters, writers and scientists whose work was inspired by their dreams.

AIM - to develop the following skills:

1. Social skills.

2. To engage in philosophical debate with their peers.

3. Comprehension – ability to understand and answer the questions on the worksheet.

4. Artistic and/or literary expression.

5. Numeracy (length of sleep) – class data could be pooled and pupils could produce a graph, work out mean, median etc....

6. Learn about how Science has addressed the same questions.

7. A rudimentary appreciation of Psychology.

8. Consideration of health issues in terms of amount of sleep needed.

Sleep & Dreaming Questionnaire

1. Why do you think we sleep?

    a)   To rest and rebuild our body   ☐

    b)   To rest and repair our brain   ☐

    c)   To keep us safe because we can't see very well in the dark.   ☐

    d)   To keep us safe from nocturnal predators   ☐

2. How many hours of sleep do you get on a weekday night?

    a)   Less than 4 hours   ☐

    b)   4 -6 hours   ☐

    c)   6 – 8 hours   ☐

    d)   9 – 10 hours   ☐

    e)   More than 10 hours   ☐

3. How do you feel if you don't get enough sleep?

    a)   Irritable   ☐

    b)   Tired   ☐

    c)   Angry   ☐

    d)   Can't concentrate on school work   ☐

    e)   All of the above   ☐

    f)   It doesn't seem to affect me   ☐

4. What's your Favourite Sleeping Position?

    a)   On your back   ☐

    b)   On your side   ☐

    c)   On your stomach   ☐

    d)   Curled up in a ball   ☐

<u>Question:</u> **Do you think sleeping position is important?**

5. We all experience sleepiness at some point during the day. When are you most sleepy during the day?

    a)   Before morning break   ☐

    b)   After morning break but before lunch   ☐

    c)   During lunch   ☐

    d)   In the afternoon   ☐

    e)   When you get home from school   ☐

6. Do you remember your dreams?

    a)   Sometimes   ☐

    b)   Always – nearly every night   ☐

    c)   Never   ☐

7. **Why do you think we dream?**

   a) To review our worries, hopes, fears etc... ☐

   b) To keep our brain active at night, so it stays alert ☐

   c) To release all the stresses of the day ☐

   d) To store new memories and connect them with old memories ☐

   e) To get rid of old memories and make room for new ones ☐

   f) To form or strengthen our personality ☐

   g) In response to physical or mental stimuli ☐

   h) For no good reason at all ☐

8. **Have you EVER dreamed about...... (tick all that apply)**

   a) A wild animal ☐

   b) A pet ☐

   c) An alien or a UFO ☐

   d) Your family ☐

   e) Flying or floating without the aid of an aeroplane etc... ☐

   f) Being chased ☐

   g) Finding new rooms in a house ☐

   h) Being lost ☐

   i) School ☐

   j) Good fairies or angels ☐

Of the things you have ticked, highlight those things that are not part of your everyday life.
(You might like to highlight them by drawing a circle round them in pencil or crayon).

Question: I wonder why they appeared in your dreams? Do you have any ideas?

Question: I wonder whether cats and dogs dream?

What do you think?

Now write down (or draw) ONE dream that you remember having.

LESSON PLAN FOR PART 1: SLEEP (Approx 45min)

Topic	Activity	Resources
Introduction to sleep 10 min	Plenary talk – what the lesson will cover and how students will be participating. Personal thoughts on sleep and dreaming. Hand out the Sleeping & Dreaming Questionnaire and ask pupils to complete **Q1-5**	**Sleeping & Dreaming Questionnaire**
Question 1 Why do we sleep? 5 min	Plenary discussion of why we sleep. Collect data. Who's correct? Answer - Everyone - explain that even Scientists don't know why we sleep. Explain the difference between theory and hypothesis. Talk briefly about Sleep Cycles and REM – and how REM was discovered	**Laminated Data Board or White Board Non-permanent felt pen**
Q 2 5min	How many hours do we need to sleep? Collect data and write onto whiteboard. **Children can use these data at a later stage to produce a frequency histogram and calculate mean.**	**Whiteboard & whiteboard pen**
Q 3 Lack of sleep? 10 min	Collect feedback and facilitate a discussion. Conclude – scientists recommend that KS2 children get at least 9 hours – that's 9 hours asleep, not sat in bed watching TV or playing computer games. Does the fact that we get irritable indicate that sleep is needed to rest and repair the brain? Has this been scientifically tested?	**None**
Question 4 Sleeping position 10 min	Collect data on different sleeping positions. Write results on whiteboard. Give each pupil a copy of Sleeping Position Table. Get children to try out the different positions and think about how each position makes them feel: • Most comfortable • Most safe • Warmest • Any other descriptors they can think of – enter into the table **Children can think about how they would present these data in the form of a graph or illustration.**	**Sleeping Position Table**
Question 5 Lark or Owl 5min	Plenary discussion. Collect data - how many owls, how many larks, how many don't know. Talk briefly about the implications of this for shift workers. Do their parents work shifts?	**Laminated Data Board or White Board**

Sleep Position Table

Name _____

Position **How it makes you feel**	On back	On side	On stomach	Curled up
Comfortable				
Warm				
Safe				

LESSON PLAN FOR PART 2: DREAMING (Approx 1h)

Topic	Activity	Resources
Introduction to dreaming 5 min	Briefly recap what was covered in last session. Quote - *Dreaming permits each and every one of us to be quietly and safely insane every night of our lives.* **William Dement**, *in 1959*	**None**
Questionnaire 5 min	Ask pupils to complete Q6-8 on the Questionnaire handed out last session.	**Sleeping & Dreaming Questionnaire**
Question 6 Who remembers their dreams? Less than 5 min	Plenary discussion. Hand count, enter data onto whiteboard.	**Sleeping & Dreaming Questionnaire White Board**
Question 7 Why do we dream? 5min	Collect data and write onto whiteboard. Any other suggestions? Lots of different ideas about this, no agreement. Psychologists, Dream workers, Therapists, Neurobiologists, Mathematicians	**Sleeping & Dreaming Questionnaire Whiteboard & whiteboard pen**
Question 8 Dream content 5 min	Collect feedback and facilitate a discussion. Add other things to the list that a number of children say they've dreamed about.	**Sleeping & Dreaming Questionnaire**
1st Question Why are those things highlighted appearing in your dream? 10 min	Introduce pupils to symbolism. Give examples	**Sleeping & Dreaming Questionnaire Show pictures to illustrate a symbol**
2nd Question Do animals dream? 5 min	Plenary discussion. Introduce pupils to the concept of REM dreaming.	**Sleeping & Dreaming Questionnaire**
Working on own dream 20 mins	Pupils can write or draw their dream. If writing, make it sound like a story – use 1st person, present tense. If artistic portrayal, pupils can paint, draw, colour, or use materials to make a collage.	**My Dream Record Sheet**

My Dream Record Sheet

Name _____

When did you have the dream? _____

Was it a good dream? _____

If one particular colour stood out, what colour was it? _____

What Title would you give your dream if it was a story?

_____

Write out or draw your dream here:

ABOUT THE AUTHOR

Joan was born in Saddleworth in the West Riding of Yorkshire. She has been working with dreams for over twenty five years, running dream workshops and attending international conferences. After gaining a PhD in Chemistry at Manchester Metropolitan University, she moved to the East Midlands to take up a post at the University of Nottingham, where she worked as a lecturer/educational consultant. She gave up her academic career in 2011 in order to follow her dream of being a full-time author and dream educator.

Other books by Joan Harthan:
'Working The Nightshift, How To Understand Your Dreams'
'Dreaming Yourself Aware'
'Grapefruit Pips'
More information can be found on her website www.docdreamuk.com

Made in the USA
Coppell, TX
22 May 2020